THE GARDEN LOVER'S GUIDE TO

Britain

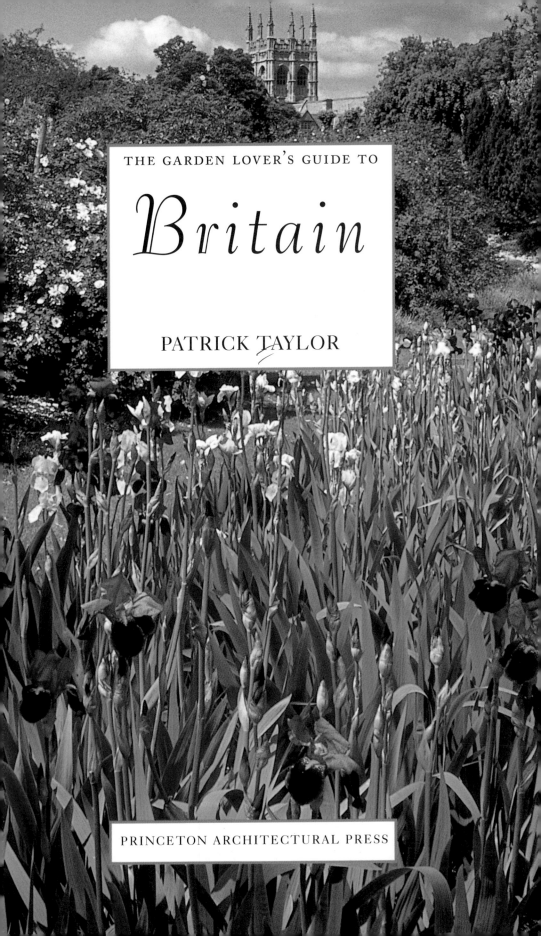

THE GARDEN LOVER'S GUIDE TO

Britain

PATRICK TAYLOR

PRINCETON ARCHITECTURAL PRESS

First published in the United States in 1998 by
Princeton Architectural Press
37 East 7th Street
New York, NY 10003
212.995.9620

For a free catalog of other books published by Princeton Architectural Press,
call toll free 1.800.722.6657 or visit www.papress.com

First published in Great Britain in 1998 by Mitchell Beazley, an imprint
of Reed Consumer Books Limited, London

Library of Congress Cataloging-in-Publication Data for this title is
available upon request from the publisher.

ISBN 1-56898-129-5

For Mitchell Beazley
Executive Editor: Guy Croton
Executive Art Editor: Ruth Hope
Editor: Selina Mumford
Designer: Terry Hirst
Editorial Assistants: Kirsty Brackenridge, Anna Nicholas
Illustrator: Paul Guest
Cartographer: Kevin Jones
Picture Researcher: Anna Kobryn
Production: Rachel Staveley

For Princeton Architectural Press
Project Coordinator: Mark Lamster
Cover Design: Sara E. Stemen
Special thanks: Eugenia Bell, Caroline Green, Clare Jacobson, Therese
Kelly, and Annie Nitschke – Kevin C. Lippert, *publisher.*

Half title page: Culzean Castle, Strathclyde
Title: Oxford Botanical Gardens, Oxon
Contents: Hidcote Manor, Gloucs

Printed in Singapore

02 01 00 99 98 5 4 3 2 1 First Edition

Contents

How to use this book

This guide is intended for travellers who wish to visit the most historic and beautiful gardens of Britain. The book is divided into five chapters covering the major regions. Each chapter comprises an introductory section with a regional map and a list of the gardens, followed by entries on each garden. The entries are accompanied by detailed at-a-glance information telling the reader about the garden's defining characteristics and nearby sights of interest. The guide also includes five "feature" gardens, specially illustrated by three-dimensional plans.

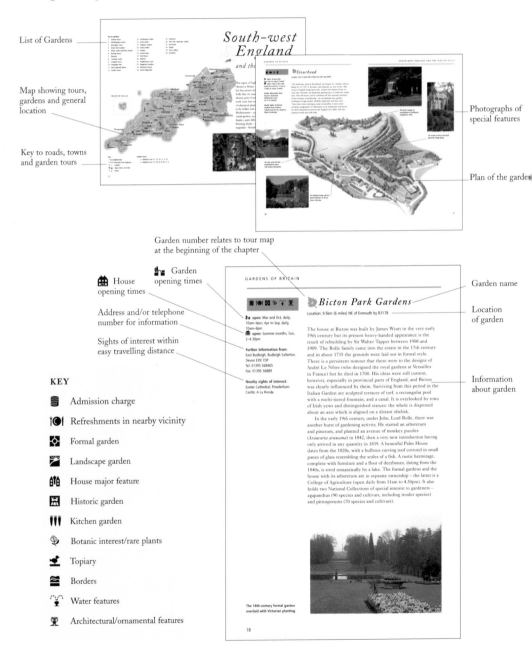

List of Gardens

Map showing tours, gardens and general location

Key to roads, towns and garden tours

Photographs of special features

Plan of the garden

Garden number relates to tour map at the beginning of the chapter

House opening times

Garden opening times

GARDENS OF BRITAIN

Garden name

Address and/or telephone number for information

Sights of interest within easy travelling distance

open: Mar and Oct, daily, 10am–4pm; Apr to Sep, daily, 10am–6pm
open: Summer months, Sun, 2–4.30pm

Further information from:
East Budleigh, Budleigh Salterton, Devon EX9 7DP
Tel: 01395 568465
Fax: 01395 56889

Nearby sights of interest:
Exeter Cathedral; Powderham Castle; A La Ronde.

Bicton Park Gardens

Location: 9.5km (6 miles) NE of Exmouth by B3178

The house at Bicton was built by James Wyatt in the very early 19th century but its present heavy-handed appearance is the result of rebuilding by Sir Walter Tapper between 1908 and 1909. The Rolle family came into the estate in the 17th century and in about 1735 the grounds were laid out in formal style. There is a persistent rumour that these were to the designs of André Le Nôtre (who designed the royal gardens at Versailles in France) but he died in 1700. His ideas were still current, however, especially in provincial parts of England, and Bicton was clearly influenced by them. Surviving from this period in the Italian Garden are sculpted terraces of turf, a rectangular pool with a multi-tiered fountain, and a canal. It is overlooked by rows of Irish yews and distinguished statues: the whole is dispersed about an axis which is aligned on a distant obelisk.

In the early 19th century, under John, Lord Rolle, there was another burst of gardening activity. He started an arboretum and pinetum, and planted an avenue of monkey puzzles (*Araucaria araucana*) in 1842, then a very new introduction having only arrived in any quantity in 1839. A beautiful Palm House dates from the 1820s, with a bulbous curving roof covered in small panes of glass resembling the scales of a fish. A rustic hermitage, complete with furniture and a floor of deerbones, dating from the 1840s, is sited romantically by a lake. The formal gardens and the house with its arboretum are in separate ownership – the latter is a College of Agriculture (open daily from 11am to 4.30pm). It also holds two National Collections of special interest to gardeners – agapanthus (90 species and cultivars, including tender species) and pittosporums (70 species and cultivars).

Location of garden

Information about garden

The 18th-century formal garden overlaid with Victorian planting.

18

KEY

Admission charge

Refreshments in nearby vicinity

Formal garden

Landscape garden

House major feature

Historic garden

Kitchen garden

Botanic interest/rare plants

Topiary

Borders

Water features

Architectural/ornamental features

Foreword

In this book I have made a severely restricted choice of just over 100 gardens of the thousands open to the public. I have chosen them both to give a true picture of the distinctive traditions of British horticulture and to recommend to visitors places that will give pleasure. But I am well aware that it is merely a glimpse through the keyhole of a vast subject. Keyholes give narrow views but not necessarily false ones. It would be true to say that in garden taste, as in many other matters, Britain is a resolutely conservative country with a sometimes almost suspicious fondness for the past. This, willy nilly, is plain in the gardens I have chosen. Quite recent gardens, such as those at Bosvigo House and at Wollerton Old Hall have a timelessness which seems to raise them from the hurly-burly of the restless pursuit of fashion. The archetypal British garden is probably the historic estate in which garden styles of several different epochs have been meticulously preserved, like layers of an elaborate and delicious cake.

Hidcote is a brilliant intermingling of lively design and fastidious plantsmanship.

Introduction

Britain has the most highly developed tradition of any country in the world of opening gardens to visitors. I have chosen a representative sample to give an idea of the very wide scope, both in terms of design and of the type of plants found. I have included all the gardens that most people would regard as the greatest gardens in the country – Hidcote, Stourhead, and so on. But I have also included many more, equally worthy of attention, showing the idiosyncrasies and astonishing inventiveness of British gardens. Charleston in Sussex (see p.50) still exudes the atmosphere of the fascinating Bloomsbury Group. Duncombe Park in Yorkshire (see p.109) shows how interested the British became in the late 18th century in the picturesque qualities of the landscape. Drummond Castle in Grampian (see p.127) displays the brilliant Scottish tradition for thrillingly decorative formal gardens. Herterton in Northumberland (see p.110), created since the 1970s, displays an idiosyncratic but disciplined style of planting of mesmerizing beauty.

Trilliums, omphalodes, and azaleas in the woodland garden at Howick Hall.

As in other countries, both the climate and history are the key to understanding gardens in Britain. With only 1,300 native flowering plants Britain has one of the less exciting floras of any European country. Yet the climate will sustain a wider range of plants than any other country, with at least 120,000 different plants, cultivars, and species grown in British gardens. The climate can vary immensely in even quite small areas. In Cornwall, for example, the hidden combes along the south coast can provide an almost frost-free environment in which exotics will flourish. Yet, on Bodmin Moor in the same county – high, cold and windy – only a severely restricted range of plants will survive. But minimum temperatures alone do not account for a plant's hardiness. Relatively cold East Anglia will permit the cultivation of many Mediterranean plants which relish low rainfall and long hours of sunshine. Such plants do not do well in the much warmer West Country which in places has a very high rainfall and restricted sunlight.

The Gothic temple and grotto in the 18th-century landscape garden at Painshill Park.

17th-century formality at Westbury Court garden.

Historically, in Britain and elsewhere, gardens follow money. A garden map shows a concentration of gardens near the centres of wealth. Although there have been great losses among houses and gardens there has been, compared with any country in Europe, an astonishing continuity of ownership. The gardens at Hatfield in Hertfordshire (see pp.58–61), owned by the Cecil family since the early 17th century, show ingredients of every period of garden history, still beautifully maintained by the family today. The same can be said of the Howards at Castle Howard in Yorkshire (see p.107) and the Cottrell-Dormers at Rousham in Oxfordshire (see p.92). Continuity of estate ownership does not ensure good gardens but it certainly aids their preservation. Britain is also uniquely fortunate to possess that marvellous organisation The National Trust which is the proprietor of the finest collection of houses, and by far the greatest collection of garden plants, in the world. Through its centralized gardens' advisory department, and the free swapping of expertise between different estates, the National Trust also conserves the most precious thing of all – the practical knowledge of gardening, often orally transmitted, without which no garden can stay alive.

The only major British contribution to international garden taste has been the 18th-century landscape garden. Gardens such as Painshill Park (see p.66) or Stowe (see pp.94–7) were on the itinerary of all 18th-century cultivated foreign travellers. They went home and attempted something similar. The other major British tradition has been the plantsman's garden, influenced by William Robinson's inspiring writings in the 19th century which encouraged a naturalistic style of gardening using hardy exotics. Gardens such as Inverewe (see p.130), Trebah (see p.40), and Kew (see p.67) belong to that tradition. But the Robinsonian tradition is still alive – as Beth Chatto's garden in Essex so vividly shows.

An 18th-century folly, built as a ruin at Mount Edgcumbe on the banks of Plymouth Sound.

Key to gardens

1 Antony House	13 Glendurgan Garden	25 Penjerrick
2 Athelhampton House	14 Greencombe	26 Prior Park Landscape Garden
3 Barrington Court	15 Hadspen Gardens	27 Stourhead
4 Bicton Park Gardens	16 Heale Garden	28 Trebah
5 Blaise Castle and Blaise Hamlet	17 Heligan	29 Tresco Abbey
6 Bosvigo House	18 Hestercombe	30 Trewithen
7 Bowood	19 Iford Manor	
8 Caerhays Castle	20 Killerton	
9 Compton Acres	21 Knightshayes Court	
10 Dartington Hall	22 Mapperton Gardens	
11 East Lambrook Manor	23 Montacute House	
12 Garden House	24 Mount Edgcumbe	

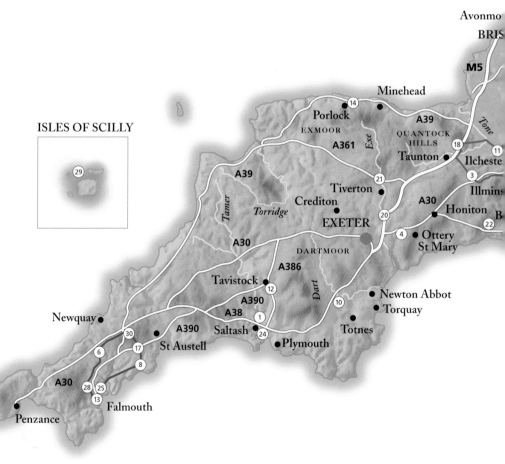

Key

═══	Motorways
═══	Principal trunk highways
③	Gardens
⬤	Major towns and cities
●	Towns

Garden tours

Northern tour: 27, 15, 23, 11, 3, 18

Southern tour: 13, 28, 25, 6, 30, 17, 8

South-west England

and the Isles of Scilly

Malmesbury
Swindon
M4
Chippenham
A4
7
19
Avon
A36
Avon
16
Mere   Salisbury
d
Stour
wn   Poole
9
Frome BOURNEMOUTH
ester
mouth

This region of England has the greatest diversity of climates in Britain. Some parts are virtually frost free but they present striking variations in other ways. The Scilly Isles, for example, have only moderate rainfall whereas parts of mainland Cornwall, especially on the south coast, have extremely high rainfall. As a collection of subtropical plants the gardens on the island of Tresco in the Scillies rival any in Europe north of the Mediterranean – and most there, too. The Cornish coastal gardens, such as Caerhays Castle (see p.21), display a quite different vegetation and the great Asiatic flowering shrubs – camellias, rhododendrons, and magnolias – flourish here. The terrain in south Cornwall is peculiarly appropriate, with steep cliffs plummeting to the sea almost in the way of a Himalayan ravine. Dynasties of Cornish gardeners – such as the Foxes at Glendurgan (see p.25) and Trebah (see p.40), or the Williamses of Caerhays Castle

Hestercombe, designed by Edwin Lutyens and Gertrude Jekyll sparkles with decorative detail.

13

(see p.21), assiduously collected rare plants, and in the 19th and 20th centuries sponsored some of the expeditions which introduced so many new plants to Western cultivation. These Cornish gardens are among the greatest treasures of British horticulture.

In the south west is rich in landscape gardens. Mount Edgcumbe (see p.34) on the coast of Cornwall near Plymouth – over 344ha (850 acres) of remarkable coastal landscape – preserves traces of a 17th-century formal garden to which a picturesque 18th-century garden has been added. Antony House (see p.16), not far away in the same county, has an exquisite park in which Humphry Repton opened cunning views running down to the Tamar Estuary – one of his most subtle designs, linking house and landscape in the most satisfying way.

In the south west 20th-century gardens of very different tendencies are well represented. Hestercombe (see p.29), in Somerset, was made just before World War I at the peak of the most productive years of the partnership between Sir Edwin Lutyens and Gertrude Jekyll. Here, the refined architecture of walls, balustrades, pools, and terraces is complemented by brilliant yet simple planting. A little later, just before World War II, Margery Fish went to live in Somerset at East Lambrook Manor (see p.24), where she devised a wholly personal style of cottage planting which has had a profound influence on garden style. In the 1950s Lionel Fortescue created a unique plantsman's garden, the Garden House at Buckland Monachorum (see p.24), in a lovely setting on the edge of Dartmoor National Park. This has been boldly expanded by his successors who have greatly enriched the garden. Lastly, at Bosvigo House (see p.20) in Cornwall, Wendy and Michael Perry, over the last 20 years, have contrived a dazzling garden of rooms with subtle planting schemes of great beauty.

Japanese irises and waterlilies in the 20th-century formal garden at Knightshayes Court.

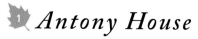

Antony House

Location: 8km (5 miles) W of Plymouth

The Carews are an ancient Cornish family who had lived at Antony for centuries before the 1720s when they built the silver granite house we see today. Before Reginald Carew-Pole consulted Humphry Repton about landscaping the park in 1792 there had been a formal garden here. Over the following ten years the grounds between the house and the estuary of the River Lynher were planted in the naturalistic fashion with groves of trees leading the eye towards distant views of the estuary.

The presiding spirit is one of informality with distinguished shrubs relishing the acid soil – especially eucryphias, magnolias, and rhododendrons. Of particular interest is the collection of daylilies, over 400 cultivars, some of which were bred here by Lady Carew-Pole. Next door to the garden is a marvellously romantic stretch of wild woodland. Views across the River Lynher include the castellated silhouette of Ince Castle on the far shore.

Athelhampton House

Location: 9km (5½ miles) NE of Dorchester

On the wooded banks of the River Piddle Athelhampton is a wildly romantic late 15th-century manor house built for the Martyn family. From the late 17th century onwards the estate declined, but in 1891 it was bought by Alfred Cart de Lafontaine who restored the house and commissioned a new garden from Francis Inigo Thomas. The garden is powerfully architectural with a series of enclosures characterized by decorative stonework, pools and fountains, lawns, and topiary.

An ornamental gate leads to the Corona, a circular enclosure which is a feast of decoration. Its wall is capped with a series of tall obelisks rising on plinths between curved sweeps of coping, and, at the centre, a circular pool is decorated with an urn and water jet. On the far side of the Corona is an enclosure featuring monumental yew pyramids, now over 10m (33ft) high, arranged about a square pool. Overlooking this garden is a raised terrace with a stone balustrade and at each end is a summerhouse with a steeply-pitched roof. The gardens at Athelhampton preserve exactly the atmosphere that the magazine *Country Life* noted in its article of 1899: "the clustered gables and battlements of Athelhampton nestle under the spreading boughs of a great cedar, and in the secluded courts can be heard the gentle coo of pigeons and the conversational patter of water."

Barrington Court

Location: 8km (5 miles) NE of Ilminster off A303

The stone manor house was built in the mid-16th century for a merchant, William Clifton. It passed through various hands and nothing is known of any garden until the early 20th century. The house was the first to be acquired by the National Trust in 1907. In 1920 it was leased to Colonel A A Lyle who was responsible for the essential layout of the garden as it may be seen today. He commissioned the architectural firm of Forbes and Tate to lay out a garden of compartments in dashing Arts and Crafts style, with finely laid brick paths in basketweave or herringbone patterns, and brick walls with stone dressings.

Plans of the garden were sent to Gertrude Jekyll who designed planting schemes. These were not followed exactly and since her day there have been further changes, but parts of the garden still reflect the lively colour sense and planting style favoured by Miss Jekyll. In the Lily Garden azaleas are planted in raised beds flanking the pool and underplanted with yellow daylilies. Later in the summer there are richer tones of *Alstroemeria aurea*, crocosmias, and brilliant red fuchsias. The former rose and peony garden was completely replanted in 1986 as a circular White Garden. The kitchen garden is divided by hedges of copper beech underplanted with red and rich pink penstemons. It is beautifully kept, a working kitchen garden, and delicious fruit and vegetables are sold from it in season.

open: end of Mar to Oct, daily except Fri, 11am–5.30pm
open: As above

Further information from:
nr Ilminster, Somerset TA19 0NQ
Tel: 01985 847777

Nearby sights of interest:
Muchelney Abbey; Tintinhull House.

The strongly architectural character reflects the garden's Arts and Crafts origins.

Bicton Park Gardens

Location: 9.5km (6 miles) NE of Exmouth by B3178

open: Mar and Oct, daily,
10am–4pm; Apr to Sep, daily,
10am–6pm

Further information from:
East Budleigh, Budleigh Salterton,
Devon EX9 7DP
Tel: 01395 568465
Fax: 01395 56889

Nearby sights of interest:
Exeter Cathedral; Powderham
Castle; A La Ronde.

The house at Bicton was built by James Wyatt in the very early 19th century but its present heavy-handed appearance is the result of rebuilding by Sir Walter Tapper between 1908 and 1909. The Rolle family came into the estate in the 17th century and in about 1735 the grounds were laid out in formal style. There is a persistent rumour that these were to the designs of André Le Nôtre (who designed the royal gardens at Versailles in France) but he died in 1700. His ideas were still current, however, especially in provincial parts of England, and Bicton was clearly influenced by them. Surviving from this period in the Italian Garden are sculpted terraces of turf, a rectangular pool with a multi-tiered fountain, and a canal. It is overlooked by rows of Irish yews and distinguished statues: the whole is dispersed about an axis which is aligned on a distant obelisk.

In the early 19th century, under John, Lord Rolle, there was another burst of gardening activity. He started an arboretum and pinetum, and planted an avenue of monkey puzzles (*Araucaria araucana*) in 1842, then a very new introduction having only arrived in any quantity in 1839. A beautiful Palm House dates from the 1820s, with a bulbous curving roof covered in small panes of glass resembling the scales of a fish. A rustic hermitage, complete with furniture and a floor of deerbones, dating from the 1840s, is sited romantically by a lake. The formal gardens and the house with its arboretum are in separate ownership – the latter is a College of Agriculture (open daily from 11am to 4.30pm). It also holds two National Collections of special interest to gardeners – agapanthus (90 species and cultivars, including tender species) and pittosporums (70 species and cultivars).

The 18th-century formal garden overlaid with Victorian planting.

Blaise Castle and Blaise Hamlet

Location: 8km (5 miles) NW of the centre of Bristol by A4108

open: Summer months, daily, dawn to dusk
open: Summer months, Sun, 2–4.30pm

Further information from:
Henbury, Bristol BS10 7QS
Tel: 0117 9506789

Nearby sights of interest:
Bath; Clevedon Court; Bristol Cathedral and the Church of St Mary Radcliffe; Wells Cathedral.

Henbury is an ancient village which, by the 18th century, had become a popular retreat for the citizens of Bristol. Blaise Hill, a wooded knoll overlooking a steep gorge, lent itself particularly well to the landscaping craze of the late 18th century. The chief estate there was bought in 1762 by Thomas Farr, who proceeded to embellish his grounds. A Gothic mock castle was built in 1766 on the brow of the hill to the design of Robert Mylne. In Jane Austen's satire on the Gothic novel, *Northanger Abbey*, Catherine Morland describes it as "The finest place in England; worth going fifty miles at any time to see." The castle today is merely a shell – but a dramatic one and it still presents a splendid goal at the summit of the hill. Later in the 18th century Humphry Repton refashioned the landscape, constructing a new carriage drive and embattled lodge on the main road from Henbury.

At the foot of the hill is Blaise Hamlet, a group of cottages designed by John Nash. The cottages are all different and display the full range of quaint architectural features – thatched or stone-tile roofs, overhanging eaves, Gothic porches, and so on. They were originally built as staff cottages for the estate. Today, kept by the National Trust, they may be seen arranged about a miniature village green with stone village pump, impeccable lawns, apple trees and informal hedges. Few places give a more vivid impression of the picturesque village landscape.

The Sham Castle: a symbol of the 18th-century English love of the Gothic.

19

Bosvigo House

Location: In the western suburbs of Truro by A390

The tradition of gardens such as Sissinghurst Castle (see p.70) and Hidcote Manor (see p.84), divided into formal enclosures enlivened by exciting planting, has proved to be a pervasive influence even in the late 20th century. Here at Bosvigo House, working since the 1970s, the owners have created a garden that is distinctively their own but pays homage to the past.

To one side of the pretty 18th-century house, concealed in woodland, are a pair of curving borders flanking a woodland path. The planting here explodes into life in late summer with a blaze of deep red dahlias, roses of a similar hue (*Rosa* 'Dusky Maiden'), golden alstroemerias, pale orange arctotis, orange lilies, and scarlet nasturtiums. Nearer the house a walled garden, overlooked by a Victorian conservatory, has herbaceous borders in red, pink, and purple and at a higher level another garden enclosed in hedges of purple plum (*Prunus cerasifera* 'Pissardii') is laid out before a classical arbour with silver, pink, and purple plants. Everywhere beautifully controlled colour harmonies enliven the scene with some rare plants playing their part in the overall effect. Some of these plants are available in an excellent small nursery.

open: Mar to Sep, Wed to Sat, 11am–6pm

Further information from:
Bosvigo Lane, Truro,
Cornwall TR1 3NH
Tel and fax: 01872 275774

Nearby sights of interest:
South Cornwall coastal scenery;
Lanhydrock; Trerice.

The Vean Garden, a carefully controlled harmony of gold and green.

Bowood

Location: 4km (2½ miles) W of Calne by A4

The architectural history of the house at Bowood is complicated. In brief, the late 18th-century British architect Robert Adam was commissioned in the 1760s to extend an older house. This house was substantially demolished in 1955 leaving some pretty fragments, including Adam's beautiful library and an orangery. The formal gardens, designed in 1851 by George Kennedy, still retain their Victorian character. But the greatest horticultural features are the landscape gardener, "Capability" Brown's 18th-century park and the 19th-century pinetum planted by the second and third Marquesses of Landsdowne. In the 1760s Brown created a lovely sinuous lake in the valley east of the house that, from certain viewpoints, has the appearance of a vast river. Concealed in the woods at the northern extremity of the lake is a spectacular cascade built to the designs of the Hon Charles Hamilton, the creator of Painshill Park (see p.66). It was actually executed by Josiah Lane of Tisbury, the great grotto builder who worked at Stourhead (see pp.36–9) as well as at

open: Apr to Oct, daily, 10am-6pm
open: As above

Further information from:
Calne, Wiltshire SN11 0LZ
Tel: 01249 812102

Nearby sights of interest:
Avebury Ring; Bath (Abbey, Georgian architecture); Corsham Court; Lacock Abbey; Stonehenge.

Painshill. The pinetum suffered in the storms of 1987, but still contains trees dating back to the original plantings.

A separate entrance takes the visitor to a 20th-century woodland and rhododendron garden (open only from mid-May to the end of June), on the northern edge of which Robert Adam's magnificent family Mausoleum commands a fine position overlooking the countryside.

 # Caerhays Castle

Location: 16km (10 miles) S of St Austell by minor roads

The Williams family is one of the great Cornish horticultural dynasties who, by sponsoring plant-collecting expeditions to the Asian hunting grounds, immensely enriched Western gardens. The site at Caerhays is a beautiful one, with the crenellated castle looking towards the sea at Porthluney Cove, and woodland giving protection from cold winds. In this benign microclimate an exceptional range of flowering shrubs are grown. This is the place for camellias, magnolias, and rhododendrons. Some of the best of these bear the family name – *Rhododendron williamsianum* and the beautiful *Camellia* x *williamsii* hybrids. A jungle-like profusion reigns here, and plants have grown to exceptional size. At the entrance to the castle a gigantic *Magnolia campbellii* flaunts its graceful sharp pink flowers. Some specimens propagated from the original seed survive in the garden. Everywhere the visitor will find incredible specimens of unfamiliar and beautiful plants grown in a wild setting that takes the breath away.

open: Mid-Mar to the beginning of May, Mon to Fri, 11am–4.30pm

Further information from:
nr Gorran, Cornwall FA1 7DE
Tel: 01872 501310
Fax: 01872 501870

Nearby sights of interest:
Bodmin Moor; South Cornwall coastal scenery; Lanhydrock; Pencarrow; Trerice.

John Nash's romantic castle, well protected by wooded slopes to the north.

Compton Acres

Location: 2.5km (1½ miles) W of Bournemouth by A35 and B3065

open: Mar to Oct, daily, 10.30am–6.30pm

Further information from:
Canford Cliffs Road, Poole,
Dorset BH13 7ES
Tel: 01202 700778
Fax: 01202 707537

Nearby sights of interest:
Kingston Lacy.

In the sedate setting of suburban Poole, Compton Acres is a remarkable collection of theme gardens arranged on a precipitous site. It was the creation of Thomas William Simpson who spent a fortune laying out the garden just after World War I. After World War II the estate was neglected and changed hands more than once but it is now finely maintained as a public pleasure garden.

The garden is divided into enclosures each of which has its own character. The Italian garden is a long canal with water lilies, surrounded by parterres of bedding plants, statues, and urns. The Japanese garden, in a narrow valley with a stream, has snow lanterns, stepping stones, bronze cranes, and many Japanese maples and azaleas. A rock garden is planted with dwarf conifers but there are other trees and shrubs such as the beautiful large-leaved tender *Rhododendron sinogrande* and the curious shrub *Desfontainia spinosa*, which produces large plum-coloured seed-pods. On the lower slopes a woodland walk is filled with azaleas and rhododendrons growing among trees. Some may find all this too self-consciously touristic but it is beautifully kept, with many good plants, and the clifftop site is particularly attractive.

A fantasy Italian garden – 20th-century formality done with a touch of panache.

Dartington Hall

Location: 3km (2 miles) NW of Totnes by A384

Dartington is one of the most remarkable places in England. Leonard and Dorothy Elmhirst bought the estate of over 400ha (1,000 acres) in 1925 and made it into a centre for progressive education and rural regeneration. The buildings surrounding the vast medieval courtyard are mainly from the 14th century. The Elmhirsts restored the Great Hall, commissioned excellent, often avant garde, building on the estate and employing a series of distinguished garden designers – among them H Avray Tipping, Beatrix Farrand, and Percy Cane – greatly embellished the grounds.

The site, in a well-wooded valley, was a very attractive one to start with, and bore striking evidence of earlier garden-making such as the Tournament Ground south-west of the house, a series of dramatically sculpted turf terraces closed by a screen of crisply clipped yew hedges. The shaping of the land must date from some 17th- or mid-18th-century formal garden. To one side is a row of clipped yew pieces – the Twelve Apostles – which was reputedly planted in the early 1800s. On the topmost terrace on the far side is a magnificent sculpture by Henry Moore (1947), a languidly reclining woman carved of limestone backed by a magnificent procession of ancient sweet chestnuts. Below the terraces to the south-east is a stately flight of steps flanked with magnolias, the work of Percy Cane. West of the Tournament Ground at the upper level are delightful woodland walks designed by Beatrix Farrand, sparkling with magnolias and rhododendrons. There are a great number of trees of interest, including several Japanese crab apples (*Malus hupehensis*), dogwoods, *Davidia involucrata* 'Vilmoriniana' and a splendid *Quercus* x *lucombeana*.

All lovers of 20th-century architecture will see much of interest as they approach the Hall, for example the Headmaster's House – High Cross House – is a sprightly essay in International Modern style (1931–32) by the Swiss architect William Lescaze, recently restored and open to the public. This mixture of architectural styles, from the medieval to the 20th-century, set in the bold, well-planted landscape gives rare pleasure.

open: All year (except 25 and 26 Dec), daily, dawn to dusk. Guided tours available

Further information from:
Dartington, nr Totnes,
Devon TQ9 6EL
Tel: 01803 862367
Fax: 01803 865551

Nearby sights of interest:
Coleton Fishacre; Dartmoor National Park.

The boldly simple 20th-century additions to the garden are in perfect harmony with the site.

open: Mar to Oct, daily except Sun, 10am–5pm; open Bank Holiday weekends

Further information from:
East Lambrook, South Petherton, Somerset TA13 5HL
Tel: 01460 240328
Fax: 01460 242344

Nearby sights of interest:
Forde Abbey; Muchelney Abbey; Tintinhull House.

Columbines, foxgloves and the flowers of the Judas tree in May.

11 *East Lambrook Manor*

Location: 5km (3 miles) N of the A303 to South Petherton

East Lambrook Manor is an icon of 20th-century English gardening, the quintessence of the cottage garden, created by the gardener who, probably more than any other, was responsible for the idea, Margery Fish. Mrs Fish came here in 1938, finding a derelict Tudor manor house of much charm. Working (not altogether harmoniously) with her husband Walter, she made an informal garden with winding paths and dense mixed plantings. She wrote a book about this experience, *We Made a Garden*, that describes removing "old beds, rusty oil stoves, ancient corsets, pots, pans" and much else from the ground, before they could get down to planting. Mrs Fish took great interest in odd forms of native plants – double-flowered primroses, white- or violet-flowered forms of meadow cranesbill, lesser celandines, and so on. She did not disdain exotic plants (such as the rarely seen white-flowered *Cercis siliquastrum*) but her heart lay in the unexplored delights of the English hedgerow. Visitors to the garden today, finely restored by new owners following a period of neglect after her death in 1969, will find the house surrounded by planting of an astonishing luxuriance. The original character of the place has been honoured with various new additions. Among these are a superb collection of hardy geraniums, one of Margery Fish's favourite plants. The garden also has an excellent small nursery.

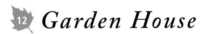

open: Mar to Oct, daily, 10.30am–5pm

Further information from:
Buckland Monachorum, Yelverton, Devon PL20 7LQ
Tel: 01822 854769

Nearby sights of interest:
Buckland Abbey; Cotehele House; Dartmoor National Park; Saltram House.

12 *Garden House*

Location: 8km (5 miles) S of Yelverton by A386

Any garden set among romantic ruins has a special appeal and the Garden House is one of the best examples. The ruins at Buckland Monachorum are those of a house built in the late Middle Ages for the abbot of nearby Buckland Abbey. The estate was bought in 1945 by Lionel Fortescue, who terraced the walled enclosure surrounding the ruins, laid out a bold structure of paths, hedges, borders, and topiary shapes, and introduced a vast range of plants. He died in 1981 since when the garden has been looked after by Keith Wiley who has added immensely to it.

To the west of the walled garden there is a new garden of quite different character. This is a giant glade of Japanese maples, a raised alpine bed, and a "ruined cottage" whose walls are densely planted. Over 7,000 species and cultivars are now grown in the garden but they are wholly integrated into a layout of the greatest charm. There is also an excellent nursery.

Glendurgan Garden

Location: 6.5km (4 miles) SW of Falmouth on the road to Helford Passage

The trump cards at Glendurgan are the site and the climate. It is situated in a narrow ravine running down to the Helford estuary and benefits from the wet, warm climate of many Cornish coastal gardens. The estate was acquired in the 1820s by the Fox family, a prominent Quaker shipping dynasty that owned several notable houses and gardens in the Falmouth area. The Foxes planted immense windbreaks and, as soon as they were established, embarked on the serious business of ornamental planting.

The valley today presents a wonderful richness of plants, many grown to huge sizes, with paths winding along the contours of both sides. The planting is almost entirely informal with one notable exception. Halfway down the valley, on its western slope, is a curious hedge maze of cherry laurel, originally planted by Alfred Fox in 1833, and recently replanted. Nearby is the rare, tender *Cunninghamia konishii* from Taiwan which demands high rainfall and a frost-free climate. Two tulip trees (*Liriodendron tulipifera*), both dating from the earliest plantings of the garden in the 1830s, have grown to well over 30m (100ft) in height – not quite the tallest in the country but certainly among the most beautiful. The spring, for magnolias and rhododendrons, is the usual season recommended for these Cornish gardens – but high summer, with the astonishing luxuriance of foliage, brings out their rare jungle-like character.

open: Mar to Oct, Tue to Sat and Bank Holiday Monday (closed Good Friday), 10.30am–5.30pm

Further information from:
Helford River, Mawnan Smith, nr Falmouth, Cornwall TR11 5JZ
Tel: 01208 74281

Nearby sights of interest:
Godolphin House; scenery of South Cornwall coast.

Alfred Fox's laurel maze (left) and *Magnolia campbellii* (right).

Greencombe

Location: 800m (½ mile) W of Porlock by road to Porlock Weir

 open: Apr to Jul, Sat to Tue, 2–6pm

Further information from:
Porlock, Somerset TA24 8NU
Tel: 01643 862363

Nearby sights of interest:
Dunster Castle; Exmoor
National Park.

The naturalistic planting at Greencombe suits the site perfectly. The garden is on a cold, shady slope and although this position severely restricts winter sunshine, very high rainfall and very little frost permit the cultivation of an extraordinarily wide range of plants. Near the house the garden is about as formal as it gets, with flawless lawns and sweeping mixed borders. Tender rarities immediately present themselves, such as a handsome bush of *Olearia insignis* from New Zealand.

West of the house paths run through woodland and everywhere there are plants to admire. Several national collections are kept here, of which the polystichum ferns provide beautiful ornament all year. Two collections of ericaceous shrubs relish the acid soil and moist climate – gaultherias and vacciniums. In spring the woodland sparkles with erythroniums. All of these plants are grown in the most natural way, happily intermingling with the native woodland anemones, celandines, and scillas, which have been in these woods forever. This garden will inform the most learned botanist and enchant any visitor.

 ## Hadspen Gardens

Location: 3km (2 miles) SE of Castle Cary by A371

open: Mar to Oct, Thu to Sun and Bank Holiday Monday, 9am–6pm

Further information from:
nr Castle Cary, Somerset BA7 7NG
Tel and fax: 01749 813707

Nearby sights of interest:
Cadbury Castle; Glastonbury
Abbey; Lytes Cary Manor.

Glaucous cabbage, *Verbena bonariensis,* and red sweet peas.

The Hadspen estate is particularly attractive with its pretty late 18th-century stone house set in parkland with wooded slopes rising behind it. The garden is at some distance from the house, in and around a beautiful walled former kitchen garden.

The Edwardian garden was much restored and enlivened by Penelope Hobhouse who lived here in the 1960s and 1970s. The garden was taken over by Sandra and Nori Pope and they have introduced, in particular, brilliantly planned colour borders disposed along the old brick walls of the kitchen garden. Down the middle a long path is flanked by mixed cream and yellow borders, backed by beech hedges. The planting is also notable for striking contrasts of shape and foliage – veils of fennel, spires of lupins, foxgloves and hollyhocks, hostas and the jagged-leafed thistle, *Eryngium giganteum.* Along the curved warm, sunny wall of the garden the predominant colour schemes modulate from intense reds and purples to pale apricot, peach, and gold. Outside the walled garden an old cistern and its surroundings have been turned to decorative use with a selection of tender plants. The attached nursery sells excellent plants.

Heale Garden

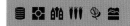

Location: 6.5km (4 miles) N of Salisbury in the Woodford valley

open: All year, daily,
10am–5pm

For many people Heale is the *beau idéal* of the English country house estate. The house, of pale pink brick and stone dressings, was built in the 17th century with crafty late 19th-century additions by Detmar Blow. Hidden from the road, it occupies a lovely position next to water meadows along the banks of the River Avon.

Further information from:
Middle Woodford, nr Salisbury,
Wiltshire SP4 6NT
Tel: 01722 782504

Nearby sights of interest:
Cranborne Manor; Salisbury Cathedral and old city; Stonehenge; Wilton House; Winchester Cathedral and old city.

Part of the garden was designed by Harold Peto, in particular the West Garden which faces the entrance to the house. From a paved area with scalloped pools a broad stone path ascends a gentle slope, flanked by an avenue of different varieties of laburnums, to a cross terrace which is lined with deep mixed borders rich in shrub roses. To one side of the house, on the banks of the River Avon, is a charming Japanese garden with an authentic tea-house and a gleaming red wooden bridge. Facing

The 17th-century house can be glimpsed above the roses and delphiniums.

it is the perfect kitchen garden in which decoration and productivity are triumphantly united. The entrance passes under a pergola draped with flamboyant roses, such as the richly scented golden-yellow 'Easlea's Golden Rambler'. Broad arched tunnels of apples and pears meet in the centre where a lily pool is surrounded by giant mounds of clipped box. Impeccable rows of vegetables are intermingled with ramparts of sweet peas, gooseberries trained into lollipops and wigwams of ornamental climbing beans. A charming summerhouse is made of pear trees pleached into a cylinder. All about the cob walls mixed borders can be found, lavishly underplanted with aquilegias, irises, hellebores, and penstemons. The garden at Heale has a marvellous peacefulness and nowhere is there the slightest trace of institutional heavyhandedness. It preserves all the character and charm of a private garden. It is as though it is your own garden and magically you have become a brilliant gardener.

open: All year except 25 Dec, daily, 10.30am–5pm

Further information from:
nr Mevagissey, St Austell,
Cornwall PL26 6EN
Tel: 01726 844157
Fax: 01726 843023

Nearby sights of interest:
South Cornwall coastal scenery;
Lanhydrock; Pencarrow; Trerice.

Heligan

Location: 6.5km (4 miles) S of St Austell by B3273

"The gardens are among the most interesting in the County, at least three generations of Tremayne fairly claiming the distinction of being described as ardent horticulturalists" wrote the *Gardener's Chronicle* in 1896. But after two World Wars the gardens at Heligan, as in so many other places, were not kept up and by 1990 had become an impenetrable jungle. Since 1991, thanks to the work of a remarkable private trust, they have been restored and brilliantly marketed under the alluring name of "The Lost Gardens of Heligan". The Tremaynes were great plant collectors and some fine old plants survived from their time. Species rhododendrons such as *Rhododendron falconeri* and *R. dalhousiae* were introduced to the West from the Himalayas by Joseph Hooker in the 1840s and the Tremayne family had seed from the first introduction.

The most spectacular part of the garden is a splendid valley garden – the Jungle – which has particularly remarkable specimens. Among these are the largest specimen of the tender New Zealand tree *Podocarpus totara* in the country and a Chinese cedar (*Cedrela chinensis*), over 30m (100ft) high and larger than any specimen known in the wild. The kitchen garden at Heligan, with its attendant glasshouses, melon- and pineapple-pits, cold frames, potting sheds and cutting borders is particularly attractive. All have been finely restored and display the workings of such gardens in their heyday. There is a cheerful razzmatazz about Heligan, not to every visitor's taste, but it does not detract from the achievement of restoring this garden to its present fine state.

The Italian Garden surrounded
with rows of cabbage palm
(*Cordyline australis*).

Hestercombe

Location: 6.5km (4 miles) NE of Taunton off A361

The collaboration between Sir Edwin Lutyens and Gertrude Jekyll produced some of the best English gardens of the 20th century but there remain few places where you can see the results of their wizardry. Hestercombe was made between 1904 and 1908 for E W B Portman who had been given the estate as a wedding present. The position is beautiful, overlooking the Vale of Taunton, but the house, as Lutyens was quick to recognize, is very ugly. His garden design takes maximum advantage of the views over the rural country drawing attention away from the house. The result is a masterpiece of shifting levels, ingenious decorative invention and masterly use of materials. All this was nearly lost – for the Portman family disposed of the estate and the house became a military hospital during World War II. However, since 1970, using Miss Jekyll's plans, Somerset County Council have brought it back to life in a pioneering restoration.

A square sunken garden, "The Great Plat", has terraces on three sides – flanked by water channels, with little beds of irises crossing the paving stones. At the head of each channel is a semi-circular pool with a mask spouting water from the niche behind. Across the southern side of The Great Plat is a stone and oak pergola garlanded with roses. Up above the eastern-most pool lies the Rotunda. Here there is an ornamental orangery and, beyond it, the Dutch Garden. Throughout the garden planting and architecture work closely together. It was always planned as a series of outdoor rooms, with plenty of places to sit from which to admire views.

open: All year, Mon to Fri, 9am–5pm; Sat and Sun, 12 noon to 5pm

Further information from:
Cheddon Fitzpaine, nr Taunton, Somerset TA2 8LQ
Tel: 01823 337222

Nearby sights of interest:
The Quantocks.

The Great Plat with idyllic views of the Somerset countryside.

open: Apr and Oct, Sun,
2–5pm; May to Sep, daily except
Mon and Fri, 2–5pm

Further information from:
Iford, nr Bradford-on-Avon,
Wiltshire BA15 2BA
Tel: 01225 863146
Fax: 01225 862364

Nearby sights of interest:
Bath; Claverton Manor; Corsham
Court; Lacock Abbey.

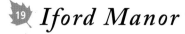

19 *Iford Manor*

Location: 11km (7 miles) SE of Bath by A36

Iford is the perfect place to observe the English passion for Classical culture and Renaissance Italy. It was the home of Harold Peto, architect and garden designer, who formed a large collection of architectural fragments and ornaments over his life. He bought Iford Manor in 1899 and reworked existing terraces behind the house, embellishing them with his collection.

Looking down these terraces there is a view that is enchanting and truly representative of English taste. Here there is a gravelled terrace with an 18th-century octagonal summerhouse at one end, and a stone wellhead and seat at the other. All along the terrace are busts on plinths, columns, sarcophagi and magnificent antique oil jars. Dense woodland presses in behind and on either side. The garden descends in steps and at the foot is an 18th-century stuccoed manor house. Beyond it there are glimpses of green pastures framed by trees with cattle grazing contentedly. The whole is uncluttered, unpretentious and utterly charming.

---

open: All year, daily, 10.30am
to sunset
open: mid-Mar to Oct, daily
except Tue, 11am–5.30pm

Further information from:
Broadclyst, Exeter, Devon EX5 3LE
Tel: 01392 881345

Nearby sights of interest:
Exeter Cathedral; Powderham
Castle; A La Ronde.

Spring in the quarry garden.

20 *Killerton*

Location: 8km (5 miles) NE of Exeter by B3181 and B3185

Sir Thomas Acland built the house at Killerton between 1778 and 1779, to the designs of John Johnson, after he had embarked on laying out his park. The house is rather dull but the grounds are exceptionally attractive. In his landscaping endeavours Sir Thomas had the help of the great nurseryman John Veitch, to whom he had let land at Budlake to start a nursery. Magnificent trees still survive from the original plantings, including sweet chestnuts, beeches, and tulip trees. Such old trees provide a superb backdrop for the profusion of ornamental shrubs and trees – camellias, magnolias, Japanese maples, and rhododendrons which subsequently flooded into the garden.

The ground slopes gently up behind the house where the planting is informal, with specimen trees and groups of shrubs in giant beds. A rustic summerhouse dating from 1831 has a delightful interior ornamented with pinecones and rattan, and the site of a former quarry has been made into a naturalistic rock garden. Near the house is the only formal part of the garden – a terrace with borders originally planted in 1900 with the advice of the great gardener and writer William Robinson. This is pretty enough but the memorable thing at Killerton is the collection of trees and shrubs, and the large setting of old parkland.

21 *Knightshayes Court*

Location: 3km (2 miles) N of Tiverton by A396

The house at Knightshayes, on a gently sloping sunny site with magnificent views, was built by William Burges between 1869 and 1874 for the Heathcoat Amory family. Burges was a late Victorian architect who specialized in highly ornate interiors. The interior at Knightshayes was never completed but the brown stone exterior has a lively decorative character.

In the 1870s Edward Kemp laid out the balustraded terrace running along the garden façade of the house and, leading off it, a yew-hedged bowling green to which was subsequently added a circular lily pond. Steps connect the eastern end of the terrace to a woodland garden developed since 1946 by Sir John and Lady Heathcoat Amory. Under a canopy of old oaks, beeches and pines they added a wealth of ornamental trees and shrubs, including magnolias, rhododendrons, *Stachyurus praecox*, southern beeches (*Nothofagus* spp.), and viburnums. An array of bulbs and herbaceous perennials provides an astonishing spring underplanting – anemones, cyclamen, erythroniums, fritillaries, narcissi, ranunculus, and scillas. Many of these are exotics but they mix easily with the native wild garlic (*Allium ursinum*) and bluebells (*Hyacinthoides non-scripta*). One of the charms of Knightshayes is that it may be enjoyed at different levels. Devoted gardeners will find plants that delight and surprise, but other visitors will love it as a piece of sculpted woodland in which the planting has been enriched and nature has been left gently at bay.

open: end Mar to beginning Nov, daily, 11am–5.30pm

open: end Mar to beginning Nov, daily (closed Fri, except Good Friday), 11am–5.30pm

Further information from:
Bolham, Tiverton,
Devon EX16 7RQ
Tel: 01884 254665

Nearby sights of interest:
Exeter Cathedral; Exmoor National Park.

In the formal garden a stone cherub shivers alongside *Erysimum* 'Bowles' Mauve'.

Mapperton Gardens

Location: 3km (2 miles) SE of Beaminster by B3163

open: Mar to Oct, daily, 2–6pm

open: Groups only, by appointment

Further information from:
Beaminster, Dorset DT8 3NR
Tel: 01308 862645
Fax: 01308 863348

Nearby sights of interest:
Abbotsbury Gardens; Forde Abbey; Maiden Castle; Parnham House.

The limestone manor house at Mapperton, mainly 16th- and 17th-century, is wonderfully decorative with twisting chimney-stacks soaring above gabled roofs and a flurry of eagles mounted on gate-piers guarding the forecourt. It lies on one side of a small valley which winds its way down to the sea. There has been a formal garden here since the 17th century but the garden today is chiefly of the 1920s. Until you are on the lip of the valley, you have no idea that a garden lies below – it bursts suddenly into view, spread out in its ornamental splendour. An orangery faces down towards the sunken topiary garden in which bold shapes of clipped yew emphasize the architecture, marking the opening of paths and following the upward progression of steps. A pool ornaments the centre with a path on either side leading to two summerhouses.

The place bristles with ornamental urns, vases and a whole menagerie of exotic creatures – griffons, herons, mermaids, and lions. The southern end of the formal garden is closed by a wall and a pergola. Beyond, the formality continues with two canal-like pools pointing towards the sea. It is possible to descend the steps and walk past the pools, pursuing the valley which becomes increasingly informal with distinguished ornamental trees – among them a splendid *Magnolia campbellii*. You may return by an upper path, from which there are wonderful views of the house poised above the formal garden and, beyond the garden walls, rural countryside with peacefully grazing cattle.

The 20th-century formal valley garden with yew topiary, bristling with ornament.

23 *Montacute House*

ocation: 6.5km (4 miles) W of Yeovil by A3088

The house at Montacute was built in the late 16th century by Edward Phelips, a successful lawyer at the court of Queen Elizabeth. Prettily set on the edge of the village the house is wonderfully seductive with richly carved local Ham Hill stone façades, curving gables and barley-sugar finials. Although there are traces of earlier layouts, the garden dates almost entirely from the 20th century.

It is entered across the former bowling green with, on one side, a magnificent billowing hedge of old yew. Beyond it is the enclosed entrance forecourt whose walls are lavishly decorated with finials. On the two corners of its eastern side are a pair of beautiful Elizabethan stone gazebos. The forecourt is lined with mixed borders, originally planted to the design of a noted local gardener, Phyllis Reiss of Tintinhull House. This is a lively arrangement of brilliant red 'Frensham' roses, dusky purple-leaved cotinus, dahlias, delphiniums, macleaya, and yucca, with repeated bushes of *Clematis recta* whose froth of white flowers gives a lightness to the whole. Beyond the forecourt a sunken garden with a balustraded pool is surrounded with rows of Irish yews and *Crataegus* x *lavallei*. A deep border running along the wall nearest the house is richly planted with shrub roses under-planted with peonies and hostas. Although the detail of these enclosures is for the most part modern their pattern suits the architecture of the great house to perfection.

open: end Mar to beginning Nov, daily except Tue, 11.30am–5.30pm; beginning Nov to end Mar, Wed to Sun, 11.30am–4pm

open: end Mar to beginning Nov, daily except Tue, 12 noon to 5.30pm

Further information from:
Montacute, Somerset TA15 6XP
Tel: 01935 823289

Nearby sights of interest:
Tintinhull House; Sherborne Abbey.

Elizabethan gazebos overlook both the borders and the former deer park.

Mount Edgcumbe

Location: 4km (2½ miles) SE of Torpoint

open: All year, daily, dawn to dusk

and Earl's Garden open: Apr to Oct, Wed to Sun and Bank Holiday Mondays, 11am–5pm

Further information from:
Cremyll, Torpoint,
Cornwall PL10 1HZ
Tel: 01752 822236
Fax: 01752 822199

Nearby sights of interest:
Buckland Abbey; Cotehele House.

The 18th-century formal garden with a parterre of cabbage palms.

The landscaper Humphry Repton was bowled over by Mount Edgcumbe, writing in 1793 that it was ". . . the most magnificent, the most beautiful, the most romantic and abounded in the greatest variety of pleasing and interesting objects." It is the ancient seat of the Edgcumbe family who, when they built their new house in 1547, sited it on a dramatic headland overlooking Plymouth Sound. The present house, rebuilt after being bombed in World War II, occupies the same position. On the slopes below it a triple avenue of chestnuts, sycamores and oaks trace the layout of a formal 17th-century garden. Walks in the woods girdle the headland, with views animated by 18th-century ornamental buildings, such as Milton's Temple, an Ionic domed building.

Formal gardens were laid out at the end of the 18th and beginning of the 19th centuries. A collection of camellias – part of the National Collection – displays no less than 470 species and cultivars. The Earl's Garden has a largely 20th-century garden of borders and walks. Fine trees survive here, including a lime dating from Tudor times, a superb Lucombe oak (*Quercus* x *lucombeana*) and the tender weeping Mexican pine (*Pinus patula*). The whole park covers an area of well over 300ha (740 acres) and offers exhilarating walks. In this balmy climate the camellias will start to flower in December, a good month in which to visit.

Penjerrick

Location: 5km (3 miles) SW of Falmouth by minor roads

open: Mar to Sep, Wed, Fri and Sun, 1.30–4.30pm

Further information from:
Budock, nr Falmouth,
Cornwall TR11 5ED
Tel: 01872 870105

Nearby sights of interest:
South Cornwall coastal scenery.

Robert Were Fox made the garden at Penjerrick in the 19th century while his brothers Charles (at Trebah, see p.40) and Alfred (at Glendurgan, see p.25) were making their gardens. Taking advantage of the mild climate and protected position he introduced immense numbers of plants. His elder daughter also took an interest in gardening, creating the Wilderness – a fantasy jungle in which cockatoos and monkeys played in a grove of tree ferns (*Dicksonia antarctica*). Later in the 19th century there was much hybridizing of rhododendrons, the famous Cornish crosses between *Rhododendron griffithianum* and *R. thomsonii*.

The charm of Penjerrick is that it preserves a secretive, almost over-grown character. Common trees provide a background for specimens of rarities, including *Amomyrtus luma* and *Eucryphia moorei*. Early in the season a walk among the densely planted groves is one of the best pleasures that Cornwall can offer.

26 *Prior Park Landscape Garden*

Location: 1.5km (1 mile) S of the centre of Bath in the village of Combe Down

open: All year, daily except Tue, 12 noon to 5.30pm, (or sunset, if earlier); closes 25, 26 Dec and 1 Jan

Further information from:
Bath, Somerset BA2 6BD
Tel: 01985 843600

Nearby sights of interest:
Bath; Bristol Cathedral and Church of St Mary Radcliffe; Wells Cathedral.

The southern edge of Bath, built on an escarpment, has fine 18th-century houses and idyllic views over the city. Here the entrepreneur and developer Ralph Allen built his Palladian villa to the designs of John Wood the Elder from 1734 onwards. The garden was started at the same time as the house, with advice from Allen's friend the poet and philosopher Alexander Pope. Today the house is a school, which it is not possible to visit, but the garden has been taken into hand by the National Trust.

It is one of the best places in England to understand the essence of the 18th-century park. The house is at the head of a steep combe running south towards the city. The valley is open but well wooded on either side where paths wind downwards. At the foot of the valley is the Palladian Bridge built by Richard Jones, Wood's successor, in 1755. It was copied from Palladio's wooden bridge on the River Brenta in northern Italy and is a delightful creation of rusticated arches, its roof supported on a colonnade with pedimented arches at either end. If you follow the recommended route – a good idea, for it gradually reveals the bridge – you will come down by the western path. Returning by the other route you will come to the beautifully restored Rock Gate. Other features remain to be restored but Prior Park is already an idyllic place, a miniature unspoilt Arcadia on the edge of urban sprawl.

The Palladian bridge (1755) – a homage to classical Italy.

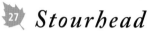

open: All year, daily, 9am–7pm (or sunset, if earlier)
open: Easter to Nov, daily except Mon and Tue, 12 noon to 5.30pm (or sunset, if earlier)

Further information from:
Stourton, Warminster,
Wiltshire BA12 6QH
Tel: 01747 840348

Nearby sights of interest:
Longleat House; Salisbury Cathedral and old city; Sherborne Abbey; Stonehenge.

Location: 5km (3 miles) NW of Mere by A303 and B3092

The landscape park at Stourhead was begun by a banker, Henry Hoare II, in 1741. It became, and remains, an icon of the 18th-century English landscape style, visited and admired from its own time onwards. As landscape gardens go it is relatively small, only 16ha (40 acres), and it combines all the essential qualities of this manner of gardening – an exceptional site, garden buildings of high quality skilfully disposed, and fine trees. There have been attempts, none successful, to trace some symbolic programme of references in its ornaments and layout. Its chief inspiration must be the English love affair with the classical world and with Italy.

The view across the lake – rhododendrons were a 19th-century introduction

The Palladian bridge with the domed Pantheon on the far shore of the lake.

The Rustic Cottage, an accumulation of architecture completed in 1806.

The Temple of Flora (1744) built above the village spring.

The house was built in about 1724 for Henry Hoare I who commissioned a suave Palladian villa from the architect Colen Campbell. Wings were later added to the pure central block with its pediments and pillars which was badly damaged by a fire in 1902. It is quite separate from the park which is concealed in a valley at some distance to the south-west of the house.

Visitors today approach the garden from Stourton Village. The Gothic Bristol Market Cross, dating from the 14th century, forms a striking punctuation mark at the garden entrance. From this point there is one of the most photographed and alluring views of any garden in England. To the left is the Turf Bridge (1762), built of stone but covered in turf. On the far bank of the lake is the domed and pillared Pantheon. Two routes about the banks of the lake now propose themselves, clockwise or anti-clockwise. One of the great charms of the garden is that most of its beauties are clustered about the edge of the lake but, partly because of its strikingly irregular shape, they reveal themselves in quite different ways according to which route you follow. For a full appreciation you should do both. The clockwise route beyond the Turf Bridge (which it is not possible to cross)

Henry Flitcroft's Temple of Apollo (1765) derived from a Roman original at Baalbec.

leads to a narrow path that passes through a shady tunnel, winding briskly uphill towards the Temple of Apollo (1765). Designed, like most of the buildings in the garden, by Henry Flitcroft, it rises up above the trees, an elaborate rotunda capped by a dome. Back down the path there is an iron bridge leading to Flitcroft's Pantheon (1754). The interior is decorated with statues, two of which (Hercules and Flora) are by the sculptor Michael Rysbrack. The columned portico is a fine place on which to stand and admire the views across the lake with the Bristol Cross catching the eye on the far bank. The path leads round into the Grotto, a three-part chamber surfaced with tufa and decorated with statues. A reclining figure of a nymph lies on a plinth with water cascading into a pool below. At the end a figure of a river god carved by John Cheere celebrates the source of the River Stour that provides water for the lake, splendidly revealed through an opening in the rocky wall of the grotto. The notion of passing from broad daylight into the shivery gloom of such a grotto was essential to the 18th-century landscaper's art.

The path now runs along the narrow northern spit of the lake, with marvellous views across it to the richly planted slopes.

Following this path round the lake it leads eventually to the Temple of Flora (Henry Flitcroft, 1744), an elegant building with a pediment supported on columns and an inscription from Virgil's Aeneid, *Procul, o procul este profani* ("Be gone, be gone you who are not believers"). Is this a warning to those unwilling to submit to the charms of the place to keep out?

The overwhelming impression of Stourhead's landscape garden is that of a series of exquisitely framed views. These views are intricately composed – buildings, trees, the lake and its invitingly grassy banks. There are magnificent trees (a superb *Liriodendron tulipifera* on an island in the lake is unforgettable) but somehow they assume the role of features in a landscape rather than objects to be scrutinized for themselves. Pictures of Stourhead dating from the 18th century show the landscape before the trees had grown and clothed the slopes surrounding the lake. A great deal else has changed – generations of the Hoare family have constantly added new plants – but the essential nature of the place has largely remained intact. Although much visited, it has the ability to absorb visitors who will always find a solitary place in which to experience Stourhead's essence.

New growth on willows brings startling colour in spring; the Temple of Flora in the background.

Further information from:
Mawnan Smith, nr Falmouth,
Cornwall TR11 5JZ
Tel: 01326 250448
Fax: 01326 250781

Nearby sights of interest:
South Cornwall coastal scenery;
Trelissick.

 ## *Trebah*

Location: 6.5km (4 miles) SW of Falmouth off A394 or A39

Trebah is another garden connected with the Fox family (see Glendurgan p.25 and Penjerrick p.34). Charles Fox came here in 1831. It is the neighbouring estate to Glendurgan so has a similar site – a narrow ravine sloping down to the Helford estuary. Fox started his garden by planting a much needed windbreak, chiefly of maritime pine. Throughout the 19th century the Fox family filled the valley with choice plantings. As World War II started the estate was broken up and the garden was then neglected. Since 1981, under new owners, it has been handsomely restored.

The beauty of Trebah lies in the luxuriant planting which may be experienced from the paths that wind along the valley. In the centre is a group of Chusan palms (*Trachycarpus fortunei*) well over 15m (50ft) high. Many other plants have grown to vast size, including spectacular ramparts of old tree rhododendrons. The gardens span 10ha (25 acres), but the diversity of planting and number of paths make it seem even larger.

open: All year, daily,
10am–4pm

Further information from:
Tresco, Isles of Scilly,
Cornwall TR24 0QQ
Tel: 01720 422849
Fax: 01720 422868

Nearby sights of interest:
Tresco island.

 ## *Tresco Abbey*

Location: By ferry or helicopter from Penzance

At Tresco an immense range of plants is grown, with a special emphasis on those of the southern hemisphere. The garden was started in 1834 by Augustus Smith, who made the best of an attractive site on sunny slopes with splendid views of the sea and the other islands. He terraced the ground, forming two chief axes – Lighthouse Walk running down the hill and Long Walk intersecting it – plus a maze of interconnecting paths.

Smith's first priority was to plant windbreaks of *Cupressus macrocarpa* and Monterey pine, some of which survive to this day. Once this protection was established he was able to embark on growing tender exotics. The planting is of an astonishing luxuriance, with substantial trees, such as *Metrosideros tomentosa*, and many palms, rising above dense plantings of shrubs and herbaceous perennials. Plants naturalize easily here and the ground is covered with groves of *Euphorbia mellifera*, the huge cranesbill *Geranium maderense*, and countless echiums and sedums. They spill over paths and tumble down the terraces but the abundance is always kept under control by the firm discipline of paths and steps. Constant new plantings are made, and the garden presents as brilliant a display of subtropical plants as may be seen anywhere in Europe.

Agaves, yuccas and aeoniums are among the plants which clothe the rocky slopes.

30 *Trewithen*

Location: 11km (7 miles) W of St Austell by A390

The gentlemanly house at Trewithen was built in 1723 from the lovely silver Pentewan stone found only in Cornwall. The grounds were landscaped in the 18th century – "with all sorts of English and foreign plants", as a contemporary account records – but their present character comes largely from the 19th-century Cornish tradition of plantsman's woodland gardens.

In 1904 George Johnstone inherited the estate and embarked on an ambitious replanting. Trewithen's name means "house in a spinney" and Johnstone added huge numbers of shrubs to the old woodland. It was his idea to plant the perimeter of lawn that extends south behind the house, and it is now fringed with rhododendrons and magnolias, some of which survive from his time. On either side of this lawn walks lead through woodland that is rich in ornamental trees and shrubs, especially camellias, magnolias, maples, and rhododendrons. There are also rarities from much less familiar genera, such as *Franklinia alatamaha* and *Reevesia pubescens*. Closer to the house are agreeable passages of formality, such as the decorative Wall Garden with tender plants like the lobster claw plant (*Clianthus puniceus*) and, a plant which was bred here, the sweetly scented, powder-blue *Ceanothus arboreus* 'Trewithen Blue'.

open: Mar to Sep, Mon to Sat, 10am–4.30pm
open: Apr to Jul, Mon and Tue, 2–4.30pm. Guided tours only

Further information from:
Grampound Road, nr Truro, Cornwall TR2 4DD
Tel: 01726 883647
Fax: 01726 882301

Nearby sights of interest:
Trelissick; South Cornwall coastal scenery.

The woodland garden in April is brilliant with camellias and azaleas.

Key to gardens

1   Anglesey Abbey
2   Benington Lordship
3   Beth Chatto Gardens
4   Blickling Hall
5   Charleston
6   Chiswick House
7   Godinton Park
8   Great Dixter
9   Ham House
10 Hampton Court Palace
11 Hatfield House
12 Helmingham Hall
13 Hever Castle
14 Longstock Water Gardens
15 The Manor House
16 Mottisfont Abbey Garden
17 Nymans Garden
18 Painshill Park
19 Petworth House
20 Royal Botanic Garden, Kew
21 Saling Hall
22 Scotney Castle
23 Sheffield Park
24 Sissinghurst Castle
25 West Dean Gardens
26 Wisley Garden

Key

≡ Motorways
— Principal trunk highways
③ Gardens
⬤ Major towns and cities
● Towns

Garden tours

—·— London tour: 6, 9, 20, 10, 18, 26
—— South coast tour: 5, 25, 19, 17

South-east England

Great
Yarmouth

This part of England has the greatest concentration of wealth in the country. The proximity of the Court, in or near London, for an immense span of history, has drawn the ambitious to the area. In addition, the ports along the south-east coast have long been an essential part of the trading link with Europe. Reputations and fortunes were made, and unmade, with bewildering speed. Great estates show much less continuity of ownership than in more rural parts of the country. Hever Castle (see pp.62–3) south of London was built into a great seat of power by Sir Geoffrey Boleyn in the 15th century. His grand-daughter, Anne, was the second wife of King Henry VIII (and mother of Elizabeth I). The estate changed hands several times and was eventually saved, and castle and garden magnificently restored, by new money in the form of the American newspaper tycoon William Waldorf Astor at the beginning of the 20th century.

Of the great estates close to London, Hampton Court Palace (see p.57), still in the possession of the royal family, preserves a remarkable ensemble of buildings dating back to the early 16th

Salvia pratensis and the rose 'Sidonie' at Mottisfont Abbey.

43

century and is one of the most fascinating gardens in the country. Its setting, on a relatively unspoilt loop of the Thames, is still a marvel to see.

The climate in the area is relatively homogenous with only moderate rainfall and much sunshine. But striking variations occur the closer one gets to the south coast. A garden such as Great Dixter (see pp.52–5), which is situated on the borders of East Sussex and Kent, has a more benign microclimate than that of nearby Sissinghurst Castle (see p.70), which is further away from the sea and in a slightly more elevated position. Several gardens take marvellous advantage of their sites to create landscapes of particular interest – two stikingly contrasting examples show the range of possibilities. The Beth Chatto Gardens (see p.48) are in one of the driest parts of Britain and Mrs Chatto has met the challenge by making a superb "gravel garden", which is never watered, with Mediterranean-style plants disposed naturalistically. Longstock Water Gardens (see p.63), on the other hand, had the benefit of plentiful natural water from nearby streams flowing into the River Test. Here the opportunity has been seized to create a water garden in which moisture-loving plants find a suitable habitat in which to thrive.

Under the cultural influence of the capital many of the gardens show advanced ideas in garden taste. The area contains some exceptional 18th-century landscape gardens, such as Petworth House (see p.66), one of "Capability" Brown's earliest commissions. Remarkable 18th-century gardens were also made by gentleman-amateurs of which Painshill Park in Surrey (see p.66) is an outstanding example. Lastly, the area contains a great many superlative 20th-century plantsman's gardens such as Nymans in Sussex (see p.65), Great Dixter (see pp.52–5) and Sissinghurst Castle (see p.70).

Blowsy late-summer borders in the restored Edwardian kitchen garden at West Dean.

Anglesey Abbey

Location: 9.5km (6 miles) NE of Cambridge by B1102

open: End Mar to Jun, Wed to Sat and Bank Holiday Monday, 11am–5.30pm; Jul to Aug, daily, 11am–5.30pm; Sep to Oct, Wed to Sun, 11am–5.30pm
open: Easter to mid-Oct, daily except Mon and Tue, 1–5pm

Further information from:
Lode, Cambridge,
Cambridgeshire CB5 9EJ
Tel: 01223 811200

Nearby sights of interest:
Audley End House; Cambridge University and Botanic Garden; Fitzwilliam Museum; Ickworth.

This garden is unique, a gigantic landscape in which formality and beautiful ornaments play a significant part. It was created in the 1930s by Lord Fairhaven, at a time when English garden taste was turning to flower and cottage gardens. The abbey was an Augustinian priory dating from the 12th century and dissolved in the early 16th century. Its core is still medieval with 17th-century and 20th-century additions. Some fine trees survive from the 19th century but the garden owes almost all its distinction to the work of Lord Fairhaven.

It is a garden on the grandest scale, with 40ha (100 acres) of designed landscape and many correspondingly ambitious effects. The site is flat and the only way Lord Fairhaven could animate its surface was to lay out avenues with planned vistas enlivened by statues and urns. A quadruple avenue of horse chestnuts, the Coronation Avenue, was laid out in 1937 to celebrate the coronation of King George VI. It forms one of the great axes of the garden. The Temple Lawn, north-west of the Coronation Avenue, was made for the coronation of Queen Elizabeth II in 1953. Here a rondel of yew is ornamented by 18th-century Corinthian columns taken from the demolished Chesterfield House. At the centre is a lively white marble copy of Bernini's "Boy David" and the entrance is guarded by a pair of lead lions cast by Jan Van Nost in the early 18th century. Closer to the house are admirable flower gardens with fine collections of hyacinths and dahlias. The semicircular Herbaceous Garden is hedged in beech and contains two fortissimo herbaceous borders.

A pair of sphinxes guard the meeting point of two avenues.

Benington Lordship

Location: 6.5km (4 miles) E of Stevenage by minor roads

The estate at Benington Lordship is an ancient one, going back to before the Norman conquest. A keep was built here in the 12th century and some fine stonework survives from that period. The folly gatehouse and apparently ancient curtain wall were, however, built as picturesque ornaments in the early part of the 19th century. The house is substantially 18th century with later additions, all built of red brick. The garden is almost entirely of the 20th century but from it, at the end of a path fringed by snowdrops in winter, there are marvellous views over the parkland of the original pre-Norman estate. The site is attractively undulating, with the old castle moat playing a decorative part. West of the house a long walk forms a chief axis of the garden leading at its northern extremity to a walled kitchen garden. On the way there is a curious lead figure of Shylock underplanted with roses and clematis. To the west of the path is a splendid rock garden which has been restored in recent years.

Immediately before the kitchen garden is a cross axis which descends the slope flanked by beautiful mixed borders. This is a most attractive private garden which has a deliciously peaceful atmosphere, enlivened everywhere by good planting.

open: Apr to Aug, Wed 12 noon to 5pm, Sun 2–5pm; Sep, Wed 12 noon to 5pm; Easter, Spring and Summer Bank Holiday Monday, 12 noon to 5pm

Further information from:
Benington, nr Stevenage, Hertfordshire SG2 7BS
Tel: 01438 869668
Fax: 01438 869622

Nearby sights of interest:
London; Wrest Park; Luton Hoo; Knebworth House; Wimpole Hall.

Colourful bergamot, delphiniums, lupins and sweet Williams in the mixed borders.

open: Mar to Oct, Mon to Sat, 9am–5pm; Nov to Feb, Mon to Fri, 9am–4pm

Further information from:
Elmstead Market, Colchester, Essex CO7 7DB
Tel: 01206 822007
Fax: 01206 825933

Nearby sights of interest:
Coggeshall (Paycocke's);
St Osyth's Priory.

Ferns, hostas, irises, and candelabra primulas fringe a stream in the woodland garden.

Beth Chatto Gardens

Location: 400m (¼ mile) E of Elmstead Market

Beth Chatto made her name as a nurserywoman, especially in creating brilliant displays for the Royal Horticultural Society shows. In these she pioneered naturalistic arrangements of enchanting beauty, and the somewhat novel idea of grouping plants broadly by their habitats. She also wrote admirable books, in particular those about plants for dry or damp gardens. Her garden surrounds her own nursery which sells an immense range of plants, especially those described in her writings. The most exciting thing here is that visitors may see, brilliantly displayed, that her ideas work.

The gardens are divided by growing conditions and they are planted with a most discerning eye. A former reservoir and ditches provide moist ground for a great variety of plants including *Gunnera chilensis*, *Iris sibirica*, *Rheum palmatum*, trilliums, and countless ferns, which flourish in the shade of willows and other damp-loving trees. The Gravel Garden has been created on the site of a former car park. Here Mrs Chatto had the idea of attempting to grow as wide a range as possible of plants which would need no watering – a great challenge, for this is probably the driest part of England. Plants are grown in well-drained richly fed soil, covered in a thick mulch of gravel, disposed in sweeping beds without formality or straight lines. Repeated plantings of silver-leaved plants such as artemisias, *Atriplex halimus*, ballota, and many others, give a harmonious background to those with brilliant flowers, including scarlet *Tulipa sprengeri*, many alliums, red or pink penstemons, sharp yellow kniphofias, and orange alstroemerias. Many plants of striking habit or foliage give structural emphasis – tall mulleins, waves of ornamental grasses, and waving stems of *Verbena bonariensis*. These plants come from many different habitats in the wild but their ability to grow with little water seems also to make them natural companions in appearance, too. This is one of the most original gardens in England. These gardens are open throughout the year and a visit in any season will be immensely rewarding and informative.

Blickling Hall

Location: 24km (15 miles) N of Norwich

One of the most romantic houses in England, Blickling Hall was built in the early 17th century for a prosperous lawyer, Sir Henry Hobart. The architect of the house, Robert Lyminge, also designed a formal garden which, although much modified, remained more or less in place until the grounds were land-scaped at the end of the 18th century. In the 1860s a great new flower parterre was added to the east front of the house with steps rising to a long formal walk through woodland to a little temple, which had been put there in 1738. The parterre, which had a very intricate pattern of beds studded with topiary and standard roses, remained in place until it was transformed by Norah Lindsay in the 1930s. Today it retains only vestiges of the original layout, made much simpler with bold shapes of yew topiary – massive "grand piano" shapes and repeated giant "acorns" – forming a powerful pattern. Four square flower beds, one in each corner, are edged in catmint and bedding roses, and their centres filled exclusively with herbaceous planting, with plants graded to become larger towards the middle to form a floriferous pyramid. The two beds furthest away from the house are planted in "hot" colours and those closer to the house in cool blues, white, and pale pink. This free style of planting benefits from the firmly patterned structure.

The early 18th-century Wilderness which flanks the temple walk is full of character and hidden in it is a secret garden and a yew circle. The orangery on the southern perimeter of the Wilderness dates from 1782 and may have been designed by Samuel Wyatt. All this is memorable, but most splendid of all is the approach to the house by car. Rounding a bend in the road a scene of palatial splendour is revealed – ancient yew hedges line a walk up to the house which presents its dazzlingly decorative façade of gables, towers, elaborate chimney stacks, and stone mullioned windows.

open: Easter to Jun, Tue, Fri, Sat and Sun and Bank Holiday Monday, 11am–6pm; Jul to mid-Sep, daily, 1–4.30pm; mid-Sep to Oct, Tue, Fri, Sat and Sun, 1–4.30pm

open: Mar to Oct, Thu to Sun, 1–4.30pm

Further information from:
Blickling, Norwich, Norfolk
NR11 6NF
Tel: 01263 733084

Nearby sights of interest:
Felbrigg Hall; Mannington Hall; Norwich (Cathedral, castle, old city); Sheringham Park.

Giant topiary shapes of yew rise above rose beds edged with catmint.

This garden was a place to sit and talk passionately, an essential pursuit of the Bloomsbury group.

 # *Charleston*

Location: 9.5km (6 miles) E of Lewes by A27

On purely horticultural grounds Charleston is scarcely worth including in this book. However, the delightful 18th-century house in its rare setting with the downs sweeping up behind was the rural retreat of the Bloomsbury group, which firmly put its idiosyncratic stamp on house and garden. Virginia Woolf discovered it and wrote to her sister Vanessa Bell – "if you lived here you could make it absolutely divine." Vanessa subsequently bought it and lived here with her occasional lover the painter Duncan Grant, and with the writer David Garnett. Charleston has not been turned into a shrine but it effortlessly displays the magic of Bloomsbury. The rooms are almost all decorated by Duncan Grant and Vanessa Bell in their charmingly throw-away style and there are many pictures by artists such as Derain and Picasso.

The garden, enclosed in walls of brick and flint, has gravel paths, profuse herbaceous borders, lurching apple trees, and lumpy box hedges. Mysterious and witty ornaments by Duncan Grant and Quentin Bell rise up in unexpected places and everywhere there is a lively decorative sense – a terrace is enriched with a sparkling mosaic of broken china, some of it fine 17th-century ware. If the less solemn aspects of Bloomsbury appeal to you this is the best place to appreciate its peculiarly English charm. House and garden, now in the ownership of a trust, are beautifully cared for.

Chiswick House

Location: 6.5km (4 miles) SW of Central London by A4 and A316

Chiswick is a delightful house and a key monument in English architectural taste. The garden, too, is of great charm and importance but it has not been well cared for, falling into muddling institutional ownership. The house was designed from 1726 by the third Earl of Burlington, based on the 16th-century architect Palladio's Villa Rotonda, and created at the height of the English love of Palladianism. The 18th-century poet Alexander Pope wrote "Chiswick House has been to me the finest thing this glorious sun has shined on."

In the 1720s William Kent worked on the garden layout and it became an icon of the taste of its day. The estate passed into the Cavendish family (Dukes of Devonshire), who sold it to the local authority in 1954. The house has been well restored and is most rewarding to visit. The gardens still contain fine ornaments which, scattered among splendid cedars of Lebanon, have a distinguished flavour. Rather unexpectedly the most attractive part of the garden is the formal Victorian parterres laid out by Lewis Kennedy, which lie in front of a late Georgian conservatory. Here there are mopheaded acacias (*Robinia pseudoacacia* 'Umbraculifera'), geometric beds of clipped patterns of box and eyestopping bedding schemes. Older parts of the gardens which have been sketchily restored or recreated are still distinctly moth-eaten. But there is plenty to marvel at in this 24ha (60 acre) garden squashed between two of the nastiest roads in London.

Godinton Park

Location: 2km (1½ miles) W of Ashford by A20

To arrive at Godinton Park you cross a marvellous deer park, landscaped by Samuel Driver in the 1770s, in which the house is seen set among immemorial oaks. The house is essentially Jacobean, of mellow rosy-brown brick, with curved gables and mullioned windows. The architect and garden designer Sir Reginald Blomfield created the garden here at the beginning of the 20th century, recreating the kind of formality which the garden might have had when the house was built in the 17th century. The house is screened by architectural yew hedges, with crenellated buttresses and curving gables echoing those of the house. Behind them is a topiary garden, a lily pool fringed with willows, and an agreeably dishevelled walled Italian garden with a pool and a fountain of a dolphin and playing *putti*. All this formality suits the house well and the position of the whole, embedded in the ancient park, is strikingly beautiful.

open: Easter weekend, Jun to Sep, Sun, 2–5pm
open: As above

Further information from:
Ashford, Kent TN23 3BW
Tel: 01233 620773

Nearby sights of interest:
Canterbury cathedral and old city;
Port Lympne; Smallhythe Place.

The Italian garden and
the dolphin fountain.

Great Dixter

Location: 17.5km (11 miles) W of Hastings off A28

open: Good Friday to mid-Oct, daily except Mon, 2–5pm

open: As above

Further information from:
Northiam, Rye, East Sussex
TN31 6PH
Tel: 01797 252878
Fax: 01797 252879

Nearby sights of interest:
Batemans; Bodiam Castle; Rye (Lamb House, old town).

Both house and garden at Great Dixter tell the visitor much about English taste. The house is the quintessence of the vernacular country house of the South East, seeming to spring organically from the land, fashioned of local materials only. It dates from the late Middle Ages, built of brick with half-timbering, small-leaded windows, steeply pitched roofs covered in slender clay tiles, and tall, substantial chimneys. The estate was bought in 1910 by Nathaniel Lloyd, a successful businessman who in middle age, inspired by a passion for old houses, trained as an architect under Sir Edwin Lutyens, qualifying at the age of 64. Lloyd commissioned Lutyens to restore the house and make necessary additions. Lutyens resolved that nothing should be faked – "nothing has been done from imagination, there has been no

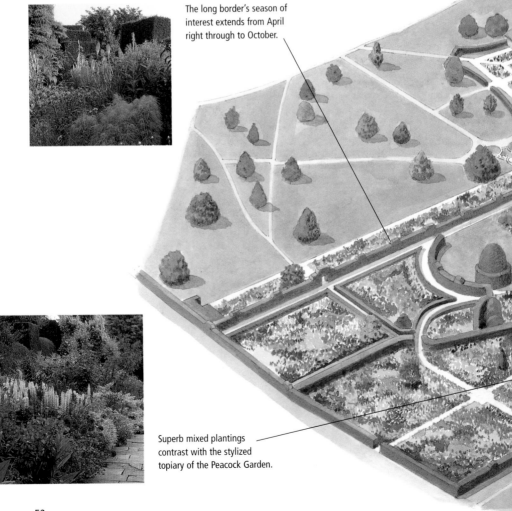

The long border's season of interest extends from April right through to October.

Superb mixed plantings contrast with the stylized topiary of the Peacock Garden.

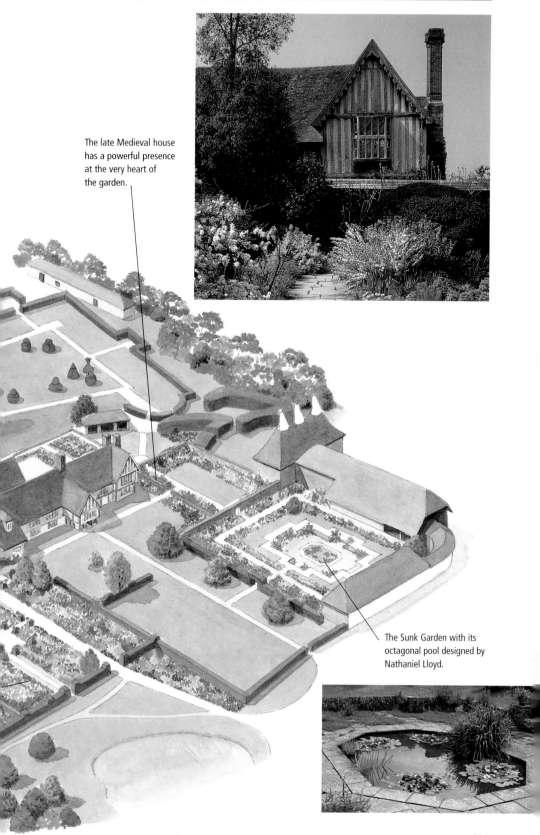

The late Medieval house has a powerful presence at the very heart of the garden.

The Sunk Garden with its octagonal pool designed by Nathaniel Lloyd.

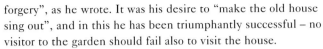

The Chilean *Cestrum parqui*, whose flowers are scented at night, flanks the doorway.

Nicotiana sylvestris, Verbena bonariensis and cannas in the Tropical Garden.

forgery", as he wrote. It was his desire to "make the old house sing out", and in this he has been triumphantly successful – no visitor to the garden should fail also to visit the house.

The site is a good one for gardening – on sunny slopes sufficiently high for refreshing breezes and close enough to the sea, 16km (10 miles) away, to provide a mild microclimate. When Lloyd bought Dixter (as it was then called) there was no garden to speak of. Lutyens was also asked to lay out a garden which he did taking full advantage of outhouses and farm buildings, some of which are as old as the house itself. He laid out a pattern of paths and hedges but Lloyd was in every way a collaborator, taking an especial interest in topiary and hedging plants. He designed the Sunk Garden (1923) and showed a fastidious interest in the use of plants for architectural emphasis. His son Christopher, born in 1921, inherited the passion for gardening and has become one of the most influential English gardeners this century. Through his books and journalism he has stimulated, inspired, and informed keen gardeners since the 1960s. His childhood home has become a test-bed for new gardening ideas which he restlessly explores to the delight of his admirers.

The house lies at the centre of the garden. The visitors' entrance is charmingly restrained, a broad stone-paved path leading from a simple gate to the gabled, overhung porch of the house. By this time you will have walked past the meadow garden, a pioneer of such things, started by Christopher Lloyd's mother. It is never cut before midsummer when it is still alive with plants which include meadow cranesbill (*Geranium pratense*), the deliciously scented meadowsweet (*Filipendula ulmaria*), and trailing blue *Vicia cracca*. The shorter grass will then allow the display of autumn crocuses and colchicums which are such a feature later in the season. Halfway down the meadow garden a right turn leads into the Barn Garden and Sunk Garden, which has an octagonal pool at its centre planted with grasses and waterlilies. The enclosing protected walls are lined with borders. Past the north-west end of the house, down steps, is the topiary lawn in which solemn pieces of yew topiary are disposed like chess pieces on an unmarked board of turf. To one side the former rose garden, laid out by Lutyens with a geometric pattern of beds, has been stripped of its roses and replaced with an extraordinary "tropical garden". In this warm and protected site there is now a fastidious jungle of all that is bold in leaf (bananas, castor-oil plants, cordyline) and brilliant in colour (begonias, cannas, dahlias) planned for spectacular late summer effect. It is a garden to be immersed in rather than merely to look at from the outside. To the south east of this is a large and beautiful informal orchard which in spring shows a dazzling collection of narcissi, a beautiful sight among the fruit blossom. From this point a set of circular brick steps ascends to the Long Border, a justly famous setpiece. The phrase "setpiece" is not quite right, for this border is the subject of endless tweaking and occasional major upheavals as Christopher Lloyd experiments with this and that. He really invented for modern gardeners the notion of the mixed border, about which he wrote his first book in 1957. This great single border is 60m (197ft) long and 4.5m (15ft) deep planted with substantial shrubs, and an endless diversity of herbaceous perennials and annuals which anticipate areas of flagging interest later in the season. A gap in the yew hedge leads through the Orchard Garden to the High Garden where there is a lovely flock of topiary peacocks riding on giant plinths.

Great Dixter continues to surprise and thrill gardeners of all kinds, and to provide wonderful lessons in the practice and aesthetics of gardening.

Helichrysum petiolare, Cotoneaster horizontalis, and *Erigeron karvinskianus* lap about the steps.

The huge shapes of banana leaves have an exotic presence in the Tropical Garden.

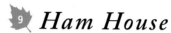

9 *Ham House*

Location: SW of Central London off the A307 at Petersham

open: Apr to Oct, daily except Fri, 10.30am–6pm (or dusk, if earlier); closes 25 and 26 Dec and 1 Jan
open: As above

Further information from:
Ham, Richmond, Surrey TW10 7RS
Tel: 0181 940 1950

Nearby sights of interest:
Osterley Park; Syon Park Gardens; Windsor Castle.

John Evelyn, gardener, diarist, and silviculturist, visited Ham House at its peak in 1678 and wrote: "After dinner I walk'd to Ham, to see the house and garden of the Duke of Lauderdale, which is indeede inferior to few of the best villas in Italy itselfe; the house furnish'd like a great Prince's; the parterres, flower gardens, orangeries, groves, avenues, courts, statues, perspectives, fountains, aviaries, and all this at the banks of the sweetest river in the world, must needes be admirable." "The sweetest river" is the Thames and visitors today can see something closely resembling the house and garden which had delighted Evelyn.

The house was built in 1610 but largely rebuilt following the Restoration in 1672. After much damage in World War II, and a long period of neglect, the National Trust acquired the estate and restored it. The garden was restored following 17th-century documents, plans, and paintings. An austere parterre of eight square lawns extends below a terrace and beyond it lies a wilderness of hornbeam hedges and field maples, and flowery meadows with anemones, cowslips, daffodils, and ragged robin. Here there are pavilions with conical roofs capped with gleaming gold balls. To one side of the house the East Court has tunnels of hornbeam surrounding a parterre of diamond-shaped beds edged with box and filled with santolina and lavender. From its windows on the east side there are beautiful views of the East Court parterre; exactly, no doubt, as was intended in the 17th century.

A recreated 17th-century parterre of box, lavender, and santolina.

10 *Hampton Court Palace*

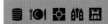

Location: 9.5km (6 miles) SW of Central London at the junction of the A308 and A309

Hampton Court's position on the banks of the Thames is still extraordinarily unspoilt and the palace buildings marvellously evocative of their time. The early Tudor palace of Henry VIII merges with Christopher Wren's late 17th-century additions for William III. The gardens have had an unhappy recent history but this is changing and in 1995 the Privy Garden was triumphantly reinstated. Lying between Wren's palace and the river, this was originally created for William III. Meticulous archaeological analysis of the site and research into the voluminous palace archives and contemporary gardening books has resulted in a dazzling and authentic reconstruction. Raised walks on either side are lined with rows of yew cones and below them are racy parterres on either side of a central walk leading to a circular pool and fountain. Wrought iron screens, dating from William III's time, are still in place but now they are fully visible as the climax to the Privy Garden, with views of the river beyond.

There is much else at Hampton Court, including the splendid, if dog-eared, remains of Charles II's formal garden of avenues, and the site of Henry VIII's garden.

open: All year, daily, dawn to dusk

open: Mid-Mar to mid-Oct, Mon, 10.15am–6pm, Tue to Sun, 9.30am–6pm; mid-Oct to mid-Mar, Mon, 10.30am–4.30pm, Tue to Sun, 9.30am–4.30pm

Further information from:
East Molesey, Surrey KT8 9AU
Tel: 0181 781 9500
Fax: 0181 781 9509

Nearby sights of interest:
Osterley Park; Syon Park Gardens; Windsor Castle.

The Privy Garden meticulously restored to its state at the end of the 17th century.

Hatfield House

Location: 32km (20 miles) N of London by A1

open: Easter to mid-Oct, daily (closes Good Friday), 11am–6pm; East Garden open Mon only (closes Bank Holiday Monday)

open: Same months as gardens, Tue to Sat except Mon and Good Friday, 12 noon to 5pm (Sun opens 1.30pm)

Further information from:
Hatfield, Hertfordshire AL9 5NQ
Tel: 01707 262823
Fax: 01707 275719

Nearby sights of interest:
Knebworth; Luton Hoo;
Woburn Abbey.

Hatfield is one of the best documented, and most attractive, of all historic gardens in Britain. The Cecil family rose to prominence as courtiers to Queen Elizabeth I in the 16th century and Robert Cecil (later Lord Burghley) built the house at Hatfield from 1607 onwards. From the start he turned his attention to the garden, bringing with him Mountain Jennings, the gardener at his former estate of Theobalds. A little later, in 1610, a key horticultural figure of the 17th century, John Tradescant the Elder, also came to work at Hatfield. He later worked for other aristocratic patrons and in due course became royal gardener to King Charles I. He was one of the pioneer plant collectors, travelling widely in Europe and North America. Archives at Hatfield House still preserve bills from this period and notes on Tradescant's plant

Delphiniums, lavatera, peonies, and geraniums in bloom in the Privy Garden.

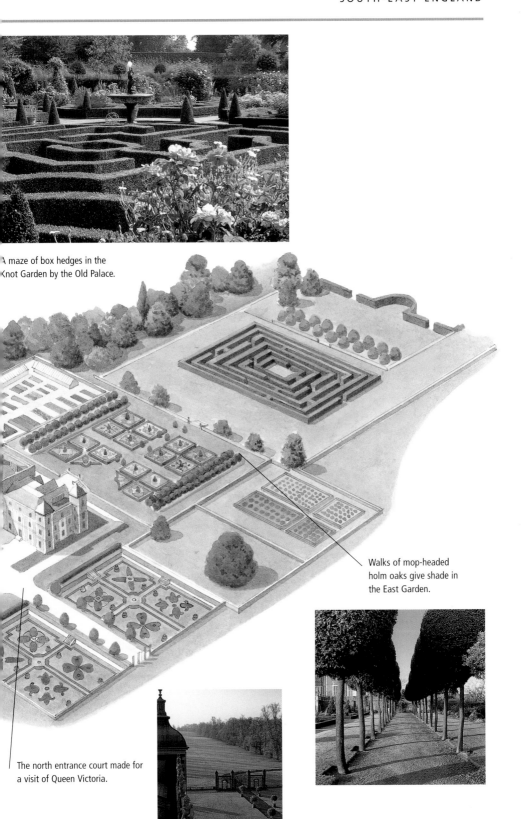

A maze of box hedges in the Knot Garden by the Old Palace.

Walks of mop-headed holm oaks give shade in the East Garden.

The north entrance court made for a visit of Queen Victoria.

59

acquisitions – "two fyg trees in an other basket called whit fygs withe manye other Rare shrubs given me by Master Robyns." This was Jean Robin, the director of the *Jardin du Roi* in Paris and gardener to the king, Henri III. Under Tradescant a flood of plants came to Hatfield, some of them tender exotics such as myrtles and oleanders. Tradescant's role was very much that of plant connoisseur and the laying out of the garden was left to other hands. Salomon de Caus, the French garden designer and maker of ingenious water-driven garden ornaments, created a water parterre with a grotto and banqueting house.

After the major gardening activities at Hatfield in the early part of the 17th century there then followed a quiet period. In the 18th century the garden was landscaped up to the very walls of the house. By the late 18th century the head of the family (now Lord Salisbury) did not live there and the estate was a sorry sight. A visitor in 1770 described "excessive neglect . . . the whole being overrun with molehills." In the 19th century Hatfield flourished once again. The second Marquess of Salisbury, anticipating a visit by Queen Victoria in 1846, made great changes, including the restoration of many features of a formal kind which were then coming back into fashion. There were other changes later in the century and in the 20th century but, from the point of view of the appearance of the gardens today, by far the most important event has been the arrival of

Foxgloves, geraniums, roses, and poppies in the borders of the Privy Garden.

the present Marchioness of Salisbury in 1982. Lady Salisbury had cut her horticultural teeth on another Cecil garden, Cranborne in Dorset. At Hatfield she had an immensely large canvas on which to work. What she has done, in general, is to honour the historic past and create a distinctly 20th-century garden. To the east of the Old Palace she laid out a Knot Garden, an intricate pattern of beds hedged in box. The garden is surrounded on three sides by a raised walk so that visitors can best admire the floriferous patterns spread out below. Much of the detailed planting is of plants known in early gardens, among them several that Tradescant introduced or grew. Here are old cultivars of narcissi, tulips, and primroses and such ancient roses as the apothecary's rose (*Rosa gallica* var. *officinalis*), and the Jacobite rose (*R.* x *alba* 'Alba Maxima'). It is fascinating to see these old plants grown together for it makes one aware of how ugly many modern forms and colour are.

The late 15th-century Old Palace with new formal gardens.

The Knot Garden is an entirely new creation of Lady Salisbury's. But the Privy Garden, which dates back to the first gardens here, preserves features of different periods. In the 18th century an enclosing walk of pleached limes was made which still gives shade on a sunny day. In the 19th century Lady Gwendolen Cecil added hedges and topiary of yew. The beds were completely replanted in the 1980s with mixed schemes, herbaceous underplantings of delphiniums, geraniums, lilies, and peonies spreading among shrub roses, many of which are the famous breeder David Austin's English Roses.

The Knot Garden evokes styles of the past with a collection of period plants.

The east gardens – open only on Monday – also combine the historic and the new. Immediately below the façade of the house is a paved terrace from where a double staircase leads down into the garden. Here, where in the 19th century there was a fussy arrangement of beds, Lady Salisbury has laid out a symmetrical arrangement of eight box-edged beds filled with decorative mixed planting. On either side are shady walks of holm oak (*Quercus ilex*) clipped into lollipop shapes and the whole garden is animated by Italian statues. Beyond it lies the Victorian yew maze created for Queen Victoria's visit.

There is a great deal else to see at Hatfield and one further point is of special interest to gardeners today. The whole garden is maintained organically and you will not often see a garden that looks more flourishing.

Helmingham Hall

Location: 14.5km (9 miles) N of Ipswich by B1077

open: End of Apr to beginning of Sep, Sun, 2–6pm

Further information from:
nr Stowmarket, Suffolk IP14 6EF
Tel: 01473 890363
Fax: 01473 890776

Nearby sights of interest:
Birdwatching on the Suffolk coast; Framlingham Castle; Ickworth.

Musk roses flank the entrance to the former kitchen garden.

The early 16th-century house and its exquisite gardens, both set in unspoilt parkland, are unforgettable. The house, prettily patterned in two colours of brick, was built for the Tollemache family who still live there. It is moated and has an adjacent moated vegetable garden which has now been turned over to decorative purposes. The pleasure gardens are almost entirely 20th century and owe much to the present Lady Tollemache.

The former kitchen garden has a chief axis pointing towards the house and is flanked with finely kept herbaceous borders. Cross axes, sometimes of tunnels garlanded with runner beans, sweet peas, or gourds, make decorative reference to the garden's culinary past. Between the kitchen garden and the house is a parterre-like rose garden with a collection of Hybrid Musk roses. There are more roses, mostly old shrub roses, in a knot garden on an ancient garden site to the far side of the house. The beds are edged with box, the first sequence filled with herbs and old garden plants, and the second with roses, which are trained into shapely bushes. There is much underplanting – blue or white *Campanula persicifolia*, catmint, cranesbills, and lavender. The garden is particularly lovely in early and midsummer when the fortissimo scent of roses is exquisite.

Hever Castle

Location: 5km (3 miles) SE of Edenbridge by minor roads

open: Mar to Nov, daily, 11am–6pm
open: As above

Further information from:
nr Edenbridge, Kent TN8 7NG
Tel: 01732 865224
Fax: 01732 866796

Nearby sights of interest:
Chartwell; Ightham Mote; Knole; Penshurst Place; Standen; Wakehurst Place.

Hever Castle is a delicious sandstone fortified manor house rising foursquare from its moat. The heart of the house was built in 1384 by Sir John de Cobham. It was bought in the 15th century by Sir Geoffrey Boleyn, grandfather of Anne, the second wife of Henry VIII. It remained substantially unaltered until it was bought this century by the newspaper tycoon William Waldorf Astor (later 1st Lord Astor). He transformed the castle but, as Pevsner noted, "Nowhere is Edwardian craftsmanship displayed with more extravagant panache, yet without damaging the medieval exterior."

There had been no gardens of note and Astor embarked on new schemes on a gigantic scale to the east of the castle. Here is an elaborate yew hedge maze and a menagerie of topiary figures. The Italian Garden is an immense walled enclosure designed to display part of Astor's collection of classical antiquities. The Pompeian Wall is divided by a series of stone buttresses between which are ornaments disposed in well planned flowery settings. At the far end of the Italian Garden is a giant loggia embracing pool and a fountain in which marble nymphs (carved by W S rith) besport themselves. It overlooks a 14ha (35 acre) lake, ug to Astor's orders by 800 men. All this, and other admirable ecorative enclosures, are set in beautiful rolling country, nriched by countless fine trees.

Longstock Water Gardens

ocation: 2.5km (1½ miles) NE of Longstock

or such a notably watery country Britain is strikingly lacking in vater gardens. At Longstock the garden is threaded with streams vhich flow into the River Test. It is in the tradition of the voodland garden, but with a new watery dimension. Little ridges span the streams and the islands, and banks are skilfully lanted with groups of herbaceous perennials – astilbes, arum ilies, candelabra primulas, ferns, geraniums, and hostas. The arger background to the garden is of trees and shrubs, especially hododendrons. There is much thoughtful planting: a white visteria trained as a bush overhangs a large pool whose surface s dappled with waterlilies; a bush of scarlet rhododendron lluminates a shady corner; pale blue *Iris sibirica* and sharp yellow *Primula florindae* edge an island on which stands an ornamental hatched summerhouse. The shapes and colours of plants are eflected enchantingly in the gleaming water. The gardens are mpeccably kept and offer an experience quite unlike any other.

open: Apr to Sep, 1st and 3rd Sun in each month, 2–5pm

Further information from:
Longstock, Stockbridge,
Hampshire SO20 6EH
Tel: 01264 810894
Fax: 01264 810439

Nearby sights of interest:
Sir Harold Hillier Gardens; Romsey Abbey; Salisbury (Cathedral and old city); Winchester (Cathedral and old city).

Purple or yellow candelabra
primulas and the foliage of irises
and petasites adorn the banks.

15 *The Manor House*

Location: 9.5km (6 miles) SE of Basingstoke, in the centre of Upton Grey

open: May to Jul, by appointment

Further information from:
Upton Grey, nr Basingstoke,
Hampshire RG25 2RD
Tel: 01256 862827
Fax: 01256 861035

Nearby sights of interest:
Highclere Castle; Old Basing
House; The Vyne.

**Pink peonies and grey lambs'
ears in the formal garden.**

This village estate is a shrine to the Arts and Crafts style. It was bought in 1905 by Charles Holme, editor of the art magazine *The Studio*, who commissioned a new house in vernacular style from the architect Ernest Newton. A little later Gertrude Jekyll designed the garden. When the present owners bought the Manor House at Upton Grey in 1984 the Jekyll garden had virtually disappeared and they resolved to reinstate it.

In front of the house the garden is informal, with sinuous grass paths leading past ramparts of shrub roses and drifts of herbaceous perennials to a hidden pool. The garden behind the house is terraced with drystone walls and has a formal layout.

On the top terrace a pergola runs across, swathed in aristolochia, roses, jasmine, and Virginia creeper. Below the second terrace formal raised beds are planted with a blowsy pink double peony and a scented rose which echoes it both in blowsiness and colour. At the centre of each group of these beds a square raised bed is planted with *Lilium regale*. The herbaceous beds are rich in Jekyllesque plants and her favourite *Yucca gloriosa* plays a major part. For any gardener seeking to understand the Jekyll magic this is an excellent place to start.

16 *Mottisfont Abbey Garden*

Location: 7km (4½ miles) NW of Romsey by A3057

open: Apr to Oct, Sat to Wed, 12 noon to 6pm (or dusk, if earlier); special late openings, every day 12 noon to 8.30pm, during the rose season
open: Same days as gardens, 1–5pm

Further information from:
Mottisfont, nr Romsey,
Hampshire SO51 0LJ
Tel: 01794 341220

Nearby sights of interest:
Sir Harold Hillier Gardens; Romsey
Abbey; Salisbury Cathedral and
old city.

The house at Mottisfont was a 13th-century Augustinian priory, largely rebuilt in the 18th century and changed again in the 20th century. It has a beautiful position in gently undulating ground on the banks of the River Test and the garden is magnificently wooded with beautiful specimens of beech, hornbeam, oak, and sweet chestnut. Near the river are superlative examples of London planes, three of which are well over 30m (100ft) high. Mottisfont, however, is best known for the rose garden established in the walled former kitchen garden from 1972 onwards. It houses the National Collection of pre-1900 roses and was laid out by Graham Stuart Thomas. Under his influence it became more than just a museum of old roses. Paths are lined with box hedges and there is much skilful underplanting. Thus the visitor may learn about gardening as well as about roses. In summer it is a rare sight – and the scents are unbelievably delicious.

17 *Nymans Garden*

Location: 11km (7 miles) NW of Haywards Heath by A272 and B2114

The house at Nymans is a historical puzzle – partly destroyed by fire after World War II, it has a convincing air of antiquity. In fact it was built in the 1920s by Leonard Messel and three generations of that family were responsible for the garden which is now in the care of the National Trust. Ludwig Messel came here in the late 19th century and it was he who first made his mark on the garden. He transformed the former enclosed kitchen garden – the Wall Garden – into a delightful mixture of the formal and informal. Forming a chief axis running north and south is a pair of dazzling mixed borders interrupted half-way down by a marble urn and fountain in a pool. On either side behind the borders are trees and shrubs planted in grass. Here, in the acid soil, are beautiful eucryphias (one hybrid, *E.* x *nymansensis*, had its origins here), magnolias, sweetly scented *Clerodendron trichotomum*, species of styrax, and many other beautiful rarities. Roses have long been a great feature at Nymans and the original rose garden was planted with specimens from the great rosarian Ellen Willmott's garden. The rose garden has recently been replanted along with other parts of the garden which were badly hit by the great storm of 1987. One of the worst losses was the old pinetum whch was virtually distroyed, but this has been replanted and much other damage made good. It is, like many of the best gardens, of idiosyncratic taste, reflecting the passions and fastidious style of the Messel family.

open: Mar to Oct, daily except Mon and Tue, 11am–6pm; open Bank Holiday Monday
open: Same days, 12 noon to 4pm

Further information from:
Handcross, nr Haywards Heath, West Sussex RH17 6EB
Tel: 01444 400321

Nearby sights of interest:
The High Beeches; Leonardslee Gardens; Wakehurst Place.

Yew topiary and a fine marble urn ornament the borders in the Wall Garden.

Painshill Park

Location: 1.5km (1 mile) W of Cobham by A245

open: Apr to Oct, daily except Mon, 10.30am–6pm, open Bank Holiday Monday; Nov to Mar, daily except Fri and Mon, 11am–4pm; closed 25 and 26 Dec

Further information from:
Portsmouth Road, Cobham, Surrey KT11 1JE
Tel: 01932 868113
Fax: 01932 868001

Nearby sights of interest:
Claremont Landscape Park; Savill Garden.

The Ruined Abbey, built as a picturesque ruin.

Painshill Park is a splendid triumph of private restoration which has brilliantly brought back to life a remarkable 18th-century landscape garden. Like many other parks of its time it was the inspiration of a gentleman-landscaper, the Hon Charles Hamilton, who exhausted his substantial fortune in its creation.

Today the garden is slightly reduced in size but the essential features and atmosphere of the place have been faithfully restored. Laid out on south-facing slopes above a winding lake with islands, the River Mole flows just beyond its far banks. An open Gothic temple occupies a fine position commanding views down towards the lake. With similar views, further along on the slope, is the charming Rococo extravaganza of the Turkish Tent, built in the late 1750s when such exotic garden buildings were at the height of fashion, and now impeccably recreated. On the edge of the lake is the Ruined Abbey, Hamilton's last "ruinous" folly. On an island in the lake, accessible by bridges to both banks, is a wonderfully ornate grotto. Walks about the banks of the lake, and into the woods to the west, reveal other ornamental buildings – a cascade at the head of the lake, the site of the Temple of Bacchus, a Gothic tower rearing up among trees, and so on. In a part of the country almost overwhelmed by creeping suburbanization its survival is miraculous.

Petworth House

Location: In Petworth village

open: Park, all year, daily, 8am to sunset; Pleasure Grounds, Apr to Nov, daily except Mon and Fri, 12 noon to 6pm; open Good Friday
open: Easter to Oct, daily except Thu and Fri, 1–5.30pm; open Good Friday

Further information from:
Petworth, West Sussex GU28 0AE
Tel: 01798 342207
Fax: 01798 342963

Nearby sights of interest:
Parham; Weald and Downland Open Air Museum.

The house at Petworth has a long history – the Percy family had a castle here in 1309. Daniel Defoe visited in 1722 and pronounced it "one of the finest piles of building, and the best modelled houses then in Britain". It had by then been transformed into something resembling its present appearance, having been completely rebuilt in the 1680s.

The house is long and low, slipping perfectly into the landscape. In the early 18th century there was a formal garden here, designed by the royal gardener George London. Further from the house, the park was one of "Capability" Brown's earliest commissions and remains one of his best surviving landscapes. There are 283ha (700 acres) of parkland here, all beautiful – a fine place for a long walk. While clearly a man-made landscape there is no sign of artificiality. It still possesses the serene character caught in Turner's landscapes painted here in the 1830s.

20 *Royal Botanic Garden, Kew*

Location: 11km (7 miles) SW of Central London by A3106

open: All year, daily,
9.30am–4pm; closes 6.30pm on
summer weekdays and on 25 Dec
and 1 Jan

Further information from:
Kew, Richmond, Surrey TW9 3AB
Tel: 0181 940 1171
Fax: 0181 332 5610

Nearby sights of interest:
Savill Garden; Syon Park Gardens;
Windsor Castle.

What makes Kew so attractive to visitors is its astonishing variety of ingredients. Long before it became a botanic garden this was a royal estate, with much of its character surviving from that period. George I's grandson, Frederick, Prince of Wales, lived here in the 1730s, in a house commissioned from William Kent. The Prince of Wales was a plant fanatic, introducing "many curious & forain trees and exotics" as a contemporary reported. His widow Princess Augusta appointed Sir William Chambers architect here in 1757 and he created many buildings, several of which survive, among them the lovely Chinese pagoda, a key monument in the history of *Chinoiserie*. "Capability" Brown landscaped the grounds in the 1770s and King George III loved to escape here from the stuffy rigours of court life at St James's Palace. It was he who appointed Sir Joseph Banks his adviser at Kew; who became, in effect, the first director of the gardens. Banks organized plant-hunting expeditions (he had accompanied Cook to Australia) and the collection at Kew quickly expanded. By 1789 there were 5,600 species in cultivation. In the 19th century under the directorship of Sir William Hooker, Kew became one of the greatest botanical research institutions in the world.

In the temperate house, a huge Chilean wine palm *(Jubaea chilensis)*.

Today, combining many activities, Kew is a wonderful place to visit. Its lovely site by the Thames, its great glasshouses (the Palm House, built in 1848, was a wonder of its age), its huge collection of hardy and non-hardy plants, are all of the greatest interest to visitors. The alpine house, a peculiarly British passion, contains one of the most beautiful specialist collections of plants, superbly displayed, that may be seen anywhere in the country. There are attractive oddities, too, like Marianne North's dream-like paintings of flowers from the tropical jungles of South America lining the walls of the building designed specifically to house them. Kew is the most visited paying garden in Britain but it is big enough to absorb visitors with ease. There are more than 121ha (300 acres) here and even on a perfect summer's day you can find yourself all alone in some delicious glade.

21

Saling Hall

Location: 9.5km (6 miles) NW of Braintree by A120

open: May to Jul, Wed,
2–5pm

Further information from:
Great Saling, nr Braintree,
Essex CM7 5DT
Tel: 01371 850141
Fax: 01371 850274

Nearby sights of interest:
Audley End House.

A fine 18th-century lead figure of
Flora among roses and vines.

Saling Hall is a very pretty house built in the early 17th century of fine brick with Dutch-style curved gables. The walled garden is dated 1698 and extends south-west from the rear façade of the house. A central path flanked by borders runs down the middle with, on either side, strips of lawn and borders positioned along the walls the whole length of the garden. Here is the essence of the English garden. There is formality, but cheerfulness keeps breaking through. The borders are full of roses underplanted with alstroemerias, daylilies, geraniums, peonies, and salvias. A procession of old apple trees marches along the paths on either side and a dashing 18th-century lead figure of Flora, the Roman goddess of flowers, holds the centre. You may now walk out of the walled garden to the west, where after passing through other decorative interludes, you will come to an arboretum planned like an 18th-century landscape park. The land is slightly undulating but animated by skilfully fashioned vistas with temples, statues, or urns acting as eye-catchers. Here are many birches, cedars, limes, maples, oaks, pines, rowans, and other trees, planted so as to form attractive groups. It is hard to believe that virtually all the planting of interest here has been done since 1975.

22

Scotney Castle

Location: 1.5km (1 mile) S of Lamberhurst by A21

open: Apr to Oct, Wed to Fri,
11am–6pm (or sunset, if earlier);
Sat and Sun, 2–6pm (or sunset, if earlier); Bank Holiday Monday,
2–6pm

Further information from:
Lamberhurst, Tunbridge Wells,
Kent TN3 8JN
Tel: 01892 890651

Nearby sights of interest:
Bateman's; Bedgebury; Bodiam
Castle; National Pinetum;
Pashley Manor.

There are two castles at Scotney; the romantically slumbering 12th-century remains of the moated old castle and a 19th-century gabled mansion. The latter was built between 1837 and 1844 for Edward Hussey, whose family had been there for generations, to the designs of the prolific designer and restorer of castles, Anthony Salvin. They are separated by a densely wooded romantic valley which was planned with the advice of the landscape connoisseur William Sawrey Gilpin. The old castle became a key element in the scenery, the resounding finale to views down the valley from the new castle. Below the new castle are the picturesque crags of the quarry from where the stone for the house was cut. This area today is planted with Japanese maples, rhododendrons, and magnolias, an exotic profusion among the native oaks and beech. At the foot of the slope the planting about the old castle is less exotic but a Henry Moore bronze is sited in a glade on an isthmus jutting out into the lake. Although small, in its context it has as strong a presence as the old castle in its much larger landscape.

23 *Sheffield Park*

Location: Midway between East Grinstead and Lewes off A275

The house at Sheffield Park, rising on an escarpment far above the garden, is an extravagantly decorative Gothic mansion designed in the late 18th century by James Wyatt for the first Earl of Sheffield. It was Lord Sheffield, too, who embarked on the landscaping of the grounds, using the services of both "Capability" Brown and of Humphry Repton. The series of lakes, which still lie at the heart of the park, were extended and immense numbers of trees planted. In the early 20th century, under the ownership of Arthur Soames, the planting was greatly enriched by many exotics, in particular hybrid rhododendrons, scarlet oaks, *Nyssa sylvatica*, and Japanese maples.

It is the vast expanse of water reflecting the colours and forms of plants that gives Sheffield Park its distinctive atmosphere today. The banks of the lakes are planted with trees and shrubs of different habit, foliage, and flower. Soaring swamp cypresses contrast with the pronounced horizontal growth of Japanese maples. Groups of tall Scots pines, displaying their beautiful pink-brown bark, rise among the rounded shapes of rhododendrons. There is much colour, too – the golden foliage of certain conifers juxtaposed with scarlet rhododendrons. The lakes provide the famous setpiece at Sheffield Park but deeper pleasure comes from the walks that penetrate the woodland on either side. Everywhere there are fine acid-loving trees and shrubs, and lovely plantings of decorative herbaceous perennials in vast quantities – astilbes, ferns, gentians, irises, primulas, and so on. It is all in the great tradition of woodland gardening but with a touch of Edwardian sumptuousness.

open: Mar, Sat and Sun, 11am–6pm; Apr to mid-Nov, Tue to Sun and Bank Holiday Monday, 11am–6pm (or sunset, if earlier); mid-Nov to 21 Dec, Wed to Sat, 11am–4pm

Further information from:
Sheffield Park, Uckfield,
East Sussex TN22 3QX
Tel: 01825 790655

Nearby sights of interest:
Borde Hill Gardens; The High Beeches; Wakehurst Place.

Brilliant autumn colours crisply reflected in the lake.

open: Apr to mid-Oct, Tue
to Fri, 1–6.30pm; Sat and Sun and
Good Friday, 10am–5.30pm
open: As above

Further information from:
Sissinghurst, nr Cranbrook,
Kent TN17 2AB
Tel: 01580 712850

Nearby sights of interest:
Bedgebury National Pinetum;
Smallhythe Place.

Geraniums, roses, and diascias
make a harmony of purple
and pink.

Sissinghurst Castle

Location: 3.5km (2 miles) NE of Cranbrook off A262

Sissinghurst has assumed almost legendary status, partly at least because of the flamboyantly unconventional and richly chronicled lifestyle of its makers, Vita Sackville-West and Harold Nicolson. It is remarkable, however, that this beautiful garden seems always to rise above the tittle-tattle and thoroughly earn its fabled reputation. In 1930 they bought the ruined castle and its neglected grounds. They quickly started work on the garden which was endlessly refined until Vita Sackville-West died in 1963.

It combines almost every style of gardening that has interested British gardeners in the 20th century. Crisp formality of sombre yew hedges and austere vistas are contrasted with exuberant planting – swathes of old roses and billowing masses of clematis. Among the wonderfully decorative Tudor buildings they built up a pattern of paths and enclosures, emphasizing their value as a precious background to the style of planting they loved. She was a great plantswoman, but it would be quite wrong to think of her as a plant snob. She was as acutely aware of the beauties of wood anemones and *Cyclamen coum* in the rough grass of the orchard as she was of some rare rediscovered old shrub rose. One of the singular triumphs of Vita Sackville-West and Harold Nicolson is that they made a garden whose essential spirit can be continued by their successors. Much of the planting has changed since their time but the potent magic survives, saluting the original spirit but not slavishly preserving the place like a museum exhibit. Thus, it is full of life and still gives visitors that jolt of excitement that all good gardens are able to do.

open: Mar to Oct, daily,
11am–6pm

Further information from:
West Dean, Chichester,
West Sussex PO18 0QZ
Tel: 01243 818210
Fax: 01243 811342

Nearby sights of interest:
Chichester Cathedral; Denmans
Garden; Weald and Downland
Museum.

West Dean Gardens

Location: 9.5km (6 miles) N of Chichester by A286

West Dean House was built in the early years of the 19th century to the designs of James Wyatt. The estate was acquired in the late 19th century by William Dodge James, a cousin of Henry James. William James was an Edwardian swell who loved nothing better than to entertain on a grand scale. He extended the house to the designs of the architectural firm George & Peto, and Harold Peto also worked on the garden. Among the features that survive from his time is a pergola, recently restored and replanted. The most exciting thing here is the magnificent kitchen garden. It is not one of the biggest – 1ha (2½ acres) enclosed in brick and flint walls – but it is one of the best. The whole place has been restored to the highest standards, making much use of original records. But the point here is not merely to display a kitchen garden like a museum, but to show it in action. The garden is divided into four enclosures with a splendid range of glasshouses. There is a collection of orchids, a fig house with an ancient surviving tree, a house for dessert grapes, specialist collections of cultivars of tomatoes, aubergines and chilies, and much else. A collection of fruit trees, grown in the open ground or espaliered against the walls, includes several historic cultivars. Vegetables and soft fruit are to be seen cultivated to perfectionist standards. Lastly, beautifully designed herbaceous borders enliven the walks between the beds of produce. West Dean is rich in practical information for gardeners who want to create something similar in their own plots.

26 *Wisley Garden*

Location: 9.5km (6 miles) NE of Guildford by A3, nr Junction 10 of M25

Wisley belongs to the Royal Horticultural Society and serves as a practical centre for horticulture. The RHS came here in 1904 and built up a garden in a somewhat piecemeal fashion, which has continued until recent times. However, there is now a masterplan imposing logic and harmony on a rather haphazard collection of ingredients. Furthermore, distinguished garden designers have been asked to lay out different parts of the garden.

Wisley has always been a marvellous place to study garden plants, which are all impeccably labelled, and to see regular trials of major groups of plants. Standards of practical horticulture are of the highest making it an enthralling place for anyone who has ever dug a bed, weeded a border, pruned a rose, or mown a lawn. There are admirable display gardens, a beautifully kept alpine house and other glasshouses, a vast collection of trees and shrubs (particularly those which flourish in the acid loam), and much else. Some of the earlier features have now become rare period pieces such as the rock garden made by James Pulham & Son in 1911. This is beautifully maintained and makes a wonderful place in which to wander. Although out of fashion, the rock garden is a superb way of cultivating and displaying plants which enjoy an Alpine habitat.

open: Apr to Oct, Mon to Sat, 10am–7pm; Nov to Mar, Mon to Sat, 10am–4.30pm; Sun, Royal Horticultural Society members only

Further information from:
nr Ripley, Woking, Surrey
GU23 6QB
Tel: 01483 224234
Fax: 01483 211750

Nearby sights of interest:
Clandon Park; Claremont Landscape Garden; Hatchlands; Polesden Lacey.

Broom, hostas, poppies, and ferns in the rock garden.

Key to gardens

1	Arley Hall	13	Kiftsgate Court	25	Snowshill Manor
2	Barnsley House Garden	14	Melbourne Hall	26	Stowe Landscape Gardens
3	Biddulph Grange Garden	15	The Menagerie	27	Tatton Park
4	Blenheim Palace	16	Oxford Botanic Garden	28	Tretower Court
5	Bodnant	17	Packwood House	29	Waddesdon Manor
6	Broughton Castle	18	Painswick Rococo Garden	30	Westbury Court Garden
7	Buscot Park	19	Plas Brondanw	31	Westonbirt Arboretum
8	Chatsworth	20	Powis Castle	32	Wollerton Old Hall
9	Chenies Manor	21	The Priory		
10	Cottesbrooke Hall	22	Renishaw Hall		
11	Eastgrove Cottage Garden	23	Rousham Park		
12	Hidcote Manor	24	Sezincote		

Key

━━━ Motorways
━━━ Principal trunk highways
③ Gardens
● Major towns and cities
• Towns

Garden tours

━━━ Northern tour: 3, 1, 27, 22, 8
━━━ Southern tour: 31, 18, 30, 2, 7

Central England and Wales

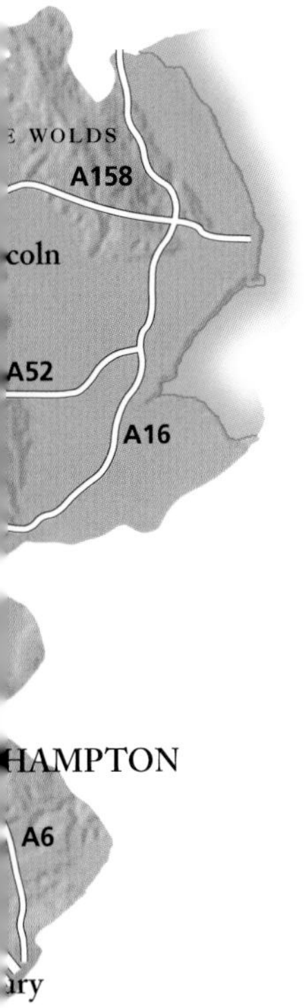

WOLDS
A158

coln

A52

A16

HAMPTON

A6

ry

The area covered in this section embraces a very wide range of climates and influences. Parts of Wales, at the westerly extreme of the region, have three times as much rainfall as the driest parts of the country and much higher temperatures than many areas. Thus, the wet and warm climate of a garden such as Bodnant (see p.79) in north Wales will permit the cultivation of rhododendrons and other tender broad-leaved shrubs, far more successfully than anywhere on the east coast. In the Midlands and Cotswolds, the climate can be extremely harsh. The coldest temperature ever recorded in England was in the landlocked county of Shropshire, far removed from the mitigating effect of the sea.

There is a confused relation between good gardens and wealth in this area. The industrial Midlands, despite the fabulous wealth generated in the 19th century, has few gardens that

The archetype of its genre – Eastgrove Cottage Garden.

owe their origin to new money. The majority of the finest gardens, on the contrary, are found in the old landed estates such as Packwood House in Warwickshire (see p.87) or Cottesbrooke Hall in Northamptonshire (see p.83). Arley Hall (see p.76), which has passed by descent since the Middle Ages, shows the fluctuating fashions of garden styles from the 18th-century landscape park to the revolutionary new herbaceous borders which were laid out here in the 1840s, setting a fashion which has dominated English garden taste ever since.

Every type of garden is to be found in the area. The single county of Gloucestershire is horticulturally one of the richest in the country. Historically this is an area of excellent agricultural land but in recent times it has, by the beauty of its landscape and architecture, attracted many garden makers. Among 20th-century gardens is The Priory at Kemerton (see p.90) with its remarkable colour borders, which are chiefly herbaceous, brilliant plantswoman's gardens such as Rosemary Verey's Barnsley House Garden (see p.77), charming oddities like Snowshill Manor (see p.93) and profoundly influential pioneer gardens such as Hidcote Manor (see p.84). Nor is it short of historic gardens, with such places as Painswick Rococo Garden (see p.88), Westbury Court Garden (see p.100), and Blenheim Palace (see p.78). Several gardens in this section belong to estates which have been owned by the same families for generations. Chatsworth (see p.81), Melbourne Hall (see p.85) and Renishaw Hall (see p.91) all remain in the ownership of the families that built them. The same is true of Broughton Castle (see p.80) where the Fiennes family still lives today. Here, as in many other historic architectural settings, the splendour of the background makes a magnificent framework for modern planting by Lanning Roper in the 1960s and, very recently, by the head gardener and the family itself.

Brilliant autumn colour from Japanese maples at Westonbirt.

Arley Hall

Location: 8km (5 miles) W of Knutsford by minor roads

Arley Hall is a Jacobean-style mansion of prettily patterned brick built in the 1830s for Rowland Egerton Warburton, whose family had owned land in these parts since the Middle Ages. There had been a garden of interest here long before the new house was built. The park had been landscaped in the 1780s by William Emes and towards the end of the 18th century the Warburtons made the Alcove Walk leading from a summerhouse to views overlooking the park. In the 1840s on the site of the Alcove Walk two herbaceous borders were laid out backed by yew hedges or brick walls, and embellished with yew topiary. This survives today and is often referred to as the earliest example of borders making use of hardy herbaceous perennials, a style much promoted later that century by William Robinson and Gertrude Jekyll. Nobody knows exactly what was planted in these borders before the 1870s but they are still a magnificent sight, with deep beds of almost entirely herbaceous plants divided rhythmically by grass paths or sculpted buttresses of yew. Also surviving from the 19th century is a handsome procession of holm oaks (*Quercus ilex*) clipped into cylinders. More recent attractions include a herb garden and a collection of shrub roses. Still privately owned and finely kept, it is the older features, however, that give Arley its distinction.

Barnsley House Garden

Location: 6.5km (4 miles) NE of Cirencester by A433 and B4425

Rosemary Verey is one of the most influential gardeners of the day. Her garden at Barnsley House, her many books and other writings, and her garden designs, have excited the interest and admiration of gardeners all over the world.

The 17th-century house is a prettily gabled Cotswold stone building. Its façade has a gentlemanly regularity that is echoed in the formality of the garden which, although rich in highly imaginative planting, is also given strong architectural shape. Much of what the visitor sees will be familiar from countless books and magazine articles – features include the intricate little knot garden, the laburnum tunnel, and a *potager*. But the detail of the planting changes constantly and Mrs Verey, apart from being a fastidious plantswoman, is also a deeply knowledgeable practical gardener. The garden is packed with ideas for planting and design from which any gardener can draw valuable inspiration.

Biddulph Grange Garden

Location: 8km (5 miles) SE of Congleton by A527

The garden at Biddulph Grange dates from the 1840s when taste was turning to all that was exotic and strange. James Bateman bought the rectory at Biddulph in 1838 and transformed it into an Italianate mansion. He was already an assiduous plantsman, having built up a collection of rare orchids at his parents home and published a book on Orchidaceae of Mexico and Guatemala. At Biddulph he collaborated on the layout of the garden with an artist and gardener, Edward Cooke.

Formal gardens to the south of the house were the first to be built, with yew-hedged parterres containing China roses. The Italian Garden, with terraces and balustrades descending to a lake, now presents a distinctly un-Italian appearance, brimming with colourful rhododendrons and azaleas. To the east of the house a Dahlia Walk was laid out, with beds divided by buttresses of yew. This has been finely restored and is a wonderful sight in late summer and autumn.

Among the most extraordinary features of the garden are those parts inspired by exotic traditions of gardening. "Egypt" is a fantasy of yew topiary – a pyramid flanked by obelisks and tiers of golden and common yew. The whole is guarded by two pairs of sphinxes. "China" is approached through a dark rocky tunnel which suddenly opens up into a Chinese temple brilliantly

open: Apr to Nov, Wed to Fri, 12 noon to 6pm; Sat and Sun, Bank Holiday Monday, 11am–6pm; Nov to 21 Dec, Sat and Sun, 12 noon to 4pm

Further information from:
Biddulph, nr Stoke-on-Trent, Staffordshire ST8 7SD
Tel: 01782 517999

Nearby sights of interest:
Little Moreton Hall.

The Chinese garden with brilliantly painted bridge and temple.

painted in scarlet, green, and gold. To the east of the house is the shady Wellingtonia Avenue, now almost entirely of deodars (*Cedrus deodara*). At its opening is an extraordinary giant stone vase of surrealistic splendour. The gardens at Biddulph were taken over by the National Trust in 1988 when, vandalized, they were teetering on the verge of extinction. A marvellous restoration has now brought them back to life.

Blenheim Palace

Location: 13.5km (8 miles) N of Oxford by A44

open: Park: All year, daily, 9am–4.45pm; Formal Gardens: Mar to Oct, daily, 10.30am–4.45pm

open: Mar to Oct, daily, 10.30am–4.45pm

Further information from:
Woodstock, Oxfordshire OX20 1PX
Tel: 01993 811325
Fax: 01993 813527

Nearby sights of interest:
Oxford (University buildings, Ashmolean Museum); Cotswold countryside; Ditchley Park.

Blenheim Palace was built between 1705 and 1725 to celebrate the military exploits of the Duke of Marlborough. Sir John Vanbrugh, followed by Nicholas Hawksmoor, created one of the great setpieces of English architecture in a landscape which is every bit as dramatic. The history of the park, in fact, goes back much further than the early 18th century. This was the site of Henry II's Woodstock Palace in the 12th century, famous for Rosamund's Bower. Although the spring from the Bower still survives, the gardens are emphatically of the later period. Vanbrugh himself, in collaboration with Queen Anne's gardener, Henry Wise, created a formal kitchen garden with bastions which was almost obliterated when "Capability" Brown landscaped the park in the 1760s. But Brown, contrary to received opinion, was sensitive to features of the existing landscape, and retained Vanbrugh's bridge and the formal vista running north from the palace of which it is part. The German traveller and garden connoisseur Prince Pückler-Muskau visited Blenheim in 1827 and wrote "one cannot help admiring the grandeur of Brown's genius . . . he is the Shakespeare of gardening". Much later, in the early 20th century, the French neoclassical garden designer Achille Duchêne was commissioned by the 9th Duke of Marlborough to create new formal gardens alongside the palace.

The Italian Garden with arabesques of clipped box and mounds of golden yew.

To the east is the Italian Garden with parterres and a fountain by Ralph Waldo Story. To the west the Water terraces have elaborate scalloped pools and Bernini's magnificent river gods fountain, a modello for that in the Piazza Navona in Rome. The new formal gardens are full of magnificent urns, ornaments and statues.

Blenheim is beautiful in winter when the palace is seen at its most theatrical, rearing up in an austere landscape. But for a full appreciation visitors must see the formal gardens and the interior of the palace. It is an ensemble which for sheer grandeur has no equal in England.

Bodnant

Location: 13.5km (8 miles) S of Llandudno by A470

Bodnant has a lovely position on the edge of the Conwy Valley from where there are beautiful views of the mountains of Snowdonia. There is no garden like Bodnant, which intermingles different garden styles to dazzling effect. Near the Victorian mansion house formality reigns, with a series of finely designed terraced gardens. These vary in flavour from the Edwardian blowsiness of the rose terrace at the top to the cool formality of the canal terrace at the bottom with its slender pool and theatrical "stage" of clipped yew hedges, statues and graceful William Kent bench. There are magnificent plants to see at every turn; from an extraordinary old *Arbutus* x *andrachnoides* at the top to an exquisite collection of mostly species magnolias.

At the bottom of the valley, running along the banks of the River Hiraethlyn, is the Dell. Here, among magnificent conifers many of which date from the first plantings in the garden in the 1870s, is a marvellous collection of shrubs grown in a naturalistic setting. Camellias, magnolias and rhododendrons clothe the slopes and the banks of the river are fringed with hydrangeas, ferns and lysichiton. If you follow the Dell to its southern extremity you may then climb the hill back towards the house. Here, by the top lawn, is a famous sight of Bodnant – the long, wide curving tunnel of pleached laburnums; an extraordinary thing to see in full flower in late spring or early summer.

open: mid-Mar to Oct, daily, 10am–5pm

Further information from:
Tal-y-Cafn, Colwyn Bay,
Clwyd LL28 5RE
Tel: 01492 650640

Nearby sights of interest:
Penrhyn Castle; Plas Newydd;
scenery of North Wales.

The Old Mill waterfall in the Dell Garden.

open: mid-May to mid-Sep, Wed and Sun, 2–5pm; in Jul and Aug, also Thu, 2–5pm
open: As above

Further information from:
Broughton, nr Banbury,
Oxfordshire OX15 5EB
Tel: 01925 262624
Fax: 01295 272694

Nearby sights of interest:
Canon's Ashby; Farnborough Hall;
Sulgrave Manor.

Box-edged beds of *fleur-de-lys* in My Lady's Garden.

 # *Broughton Castle*

Location: 3km (2 miles) SW of Banbury by B4035

Broughton Castle is a wonderfully romantic house in an exquisite setting. The stone house dates back to the 14th century but with a chiefly 16th-century appearance, retaining its moat and stunning views over ancient parkland. The Fiennes family have lived here since the 15th century but in the late 19th century it was let to Lord Algernon Gordon Lennox, one of whose garden additions happily survives. This is My Lady's Garden, which has a pattern of box-edged beds. All about them are mixed borders against the walls planted with a scheme of chiefly pink, purple, blue and white. The air in summer is suffused with the scents of roses and a profusion of plants lap against the castle walls. Alliums, mulleins, foxgloves and poppies are encouraged to self-seed but, although the atmosphere is relaxed, this is no cottage garden jumble, for the borders are beautifully kept and much art lies behind the apparent artlessness.

Between the castle walls and the moat are borders of exuberant mixed planting laid out in the 1960s by the American garden designer Lanning Roper. The castle is also well worth visiting if only for the views from the roof. From here one can see across the former deer park and straight down to the charming patterns of My Lady's Garden.

open: end Mar to Sep, Mon to Fri and every second and fourth Sat and Sun of the month, 4–6pm
open: As above

Further information from:
Faringdon, Oxfordshire SN7 8BU
Tel: 01367 242094 (not weekends)

Nearby sights of interest:
Oxford (University buildings, Botanic Gardens, Ashmolean Museum); Ashdown House; Cotswold countryside; Avebury Ring; Chedworth Roman Villa.

Buscot Park

Location: 5km (3 miles) NW of Faringdon on A417

The garden is full of interest, all of it 20th century, but the single, overwhelming feature is Harold Peto's water garden. In the walled garden the designer Tim Rees has contrived elegant plantings and nearby are richly-coloured borders, by the late garden writer and designer Peter Coats. Between the house and an ornamental lake Peto's stepped water garden makes its stately progress down a gentle incline in woodland. Hedged in box and yew, it is in the form of a stone-edged canal, studded with decorative interludes – a fountain, pools, splashing cascades and a balustraded bridge. It takes as its eye-catcher a domed, pillared temple on the far banks of the lake. Peto laid it out in the first years of this century, inspired by 16th-century gardens of Italy which he studied in minute detail. Here, at Buscot he shows that he had mastered the tricky vocabulary of sun and shade, reflective water and precisely placed ornaments.

Chatsworth

Location: 6.5km (4 miles) E of Bakewell by A6 or A619 and minor roads

The most striking thing about Chatsworth is that a house of such palatial splendour should be set down in such a remote and beautifully rural part of the country. A 17th-century poet, Charles Cotton, concluded "That this is Paradice, which seated stands/In the midst of Desarts, and of barren Sands." The barren sands today are luxuriant pastures in which cattle peacefully graze. The estate has belonged to the Cavendish family, later Dukes of Devonshire, since the 16th century, but it is only in the late 17th century that the present house and gardens have their origin. The immense house, greatly added to in the 19th century, stands on one side of the broad, shallow valley of the River Derwent.

Formal gardens were laid out in the 1690s by George London and Henry Wise and survive in part to the south of the house – the south lawn with its modern alleys of pleached lime and seahorse fountain and, continuing the axis southwards, the 250m (820ft) long canal pond. Most of the formal garden was laid out on the slopes east of the house. Of this little survives except a most enchanting formal stepped cascade and water house. The latter was designed by Thomas Archer, an elaborate fantasy down whose domed roof water tumbles. "Capability" Brown worked here for the fourth Duke in the 1760s landscaping the park to the west and laying out the splendid Salisbury Lawns to the east of the house, fringed with fine trees.

It is the work of the sixth Duke at the beginning of the 19th century that has had the most decisive influence of the garden. He recruited Joseph Paxton as his head gardener, who was responsible for the vast conservatory – or "Conservative Wall" – which runs up from Flora's Temple at the north-east corner of the house. An immense rockery, south of the cascade, also dates from Paxton's time – "The most picturesque assemblage of natural rocks" as he called it. In the 20th century much has been added, including the magnificent crinkle-crankle hedge running from the ring pond south of the Salisbury Lawns to a bust of the 6th Duke. House and garden are run as a tourist attraction – but with great brio and good sense, honouring the spirit of the place and making it marvellous to visit.

open: Easter to Oct, daily, 11am–5pm
open: As above

Further information from:
Bakewell, Derbyshire DE4 1PP
Tel: 01246 582204
Fax: 01246 583536

Nearby sights of interest:
Scenery of Derwent Valley;
Hardwick Hall; Bolsover Castle.

Attractive serpentine hedges of beech run from the ring pond.

Chenies Manor

Location: 6.5km (4 miles) E of Amersham by A404

open: Apr to Oct, Wed, Thu
and Bank Holiday Monday, 2–5pm
open: As above

Further information from:
Chenies, Rickmansworth,
Buckinghamshire WD3 6ER
Tel: 01494 762888

Nearby sights of interest:
Hughenden Manor; West
Wycombe Park.

The manor at Chenies has a long history. The present buildings date largely from the 16th century, when the estate was bought by the Russells (later Dukes of Bedford). They remodelled the old house causing the chronicler John Leland to write that it had been "so translated by Mylord Russell that little or nothing of it . . . remains untranslated." Built of brick with crow-step gables and soaring chimney stacks it preserves a romantic character. The estate passed out of the Russell family only in the 20th century; since when an admirable new garden has been made.

The house and outhouses form a fine backdrop for the lively plantings which the present owners have instated. One of the highlights of the garden year is an astonishing display of tulips, bedded out in a pretty, formal sunken garden. This is of Tudor origin but has a strong Arts and Crafts flavour with stone paving, a central pool and powerful topiary of box and yew. The tulips are planted in narrow beds about the edge of the sunken garden, arranged in blocks of colour with carefully chosen backgrounds of herbaceous plants. In late spring all the tulips are removed and a summer bedding scheme of yellow and gold argyranthemums, dahlias, Wisley primroses, rockroses and golden grass is put into place. To one side of the sunken garden a white garden of mixed borders is exceptionally successful. Nearby is a little garden of medicinal and useful plants disposed about a Georgian octagonal well-house. Still privately owned, and maintained to perfectionist standards, Chenies Manor is a delightful garden to visit.

The Tudor sunken garden with
topiary of yew and box, and
brilliant spring tulips.

Cottesbrooke Hall

Location: 14.5km (9 miles) NW of Northampton by A50

Cottesbrooke Hall was built in the early 18th century for Sir John Langham. Of rosy brick with stone dressings, it is one of the most attractive houses of its period in the country – and has gardens to match. There is beautiful 18th-century parkland with an avenue aligned with the spire of All Saints Church, Brixworth, but the chief parts of the garden date from the 20th century.

Distinguished garden designers worked here producing a satisfyingly harmonious layout. Just before World War I the architect and garden designer Robert Weir Schultz created an enclosed garden of Arts and Crafts character. Later on Dame Sylvia Crowe added a fine pavilion and in 1937 Sir Geoffrey Jellicoe laid out a sumptuously decorative formal parterre garden against the south facade of the house. Here are rounded cones of yew topiary and beds of 'Iceberg' roses enclosed in cornerpieces of yew, with urns of annuals and agapanthus adding brilliant colour among lead statues. Running along the west of the house are a magnificent pair of deep mixed borders partly shaded by ancient cedars of Lebanon. In a hidden woodland garden there is fine planting and tranquil walks on the grassy banks of a stream. There is much else to admire at Cottesbrooke and the whole estate, still privately owned, is most beautifully maintained.

open: Easter to Sep, Wed, Thu, Fri and every Bank Holiday Monday (and Sun in Sep), 2–5pm
open: As above

Further information from:
nr Northampton,
Northamptonshire NN6 8PF
Tel: 01604 505808
Fax: 01604 505619

Nearby sights of interest:
Holdenby Hall Gardens; Boughton House.

White wisteria garlands the entrance to the walled garden.

Eastgrove Cottage Garden

Location: 13.5km (8 miles) NW of Worcester between Shrawley and Great Witley

Few English gardens are so distinctively English as this. The half-timbered thatched cottage seems to grow out of the ground with organic vigour. There are few straight edges and only sketchy formality but the planting is very skilful, its abundant naturalness concealing much artistry. A bench overlooks a sea of poppies, *Eryngium giganteum*, white valerian, crimson *Cirsium rivulare* and dusky red penstemons. Nearby, an arbour swathed in yellow roses and chalk-blue clematis frames a view of grazing cows. The Morning Border flaunts red hollyhocks, and pale pink penstemons against ramparts of shrub roses. Repeated cool yellows – achilleas, hollyhocks, kniphofias and scabious – look wonderful with a background of the glaucous-grey foliage of *Rosa glauca*. Much use is made of plants in pots with subjects ranging from agapanthus to much rarer plants such as the Canary Islands foxglove. There is a delightful nursery with mostly herbaceous and frequently rare plants. All this is set in exquisite countryside.

open: Apr to Jul, Thu to Mon, 12 noon to 5pm; Sep to mid-Oct, Thu to Sat, 2–5pm

Further information from:
Sankyns Green, Little Witley,
Hereford and Worcester WR6 6LQ
Tel: 01299 896389

Nearby sights of interest:
Berrington Hall; Hanbury Hall;
Hagley Hall.

open: Apr to Oct, daily
except Tue and Fri, 11am–7pm
(closes at 6pm in Oct); Jul to Aug,
also open Tue

Further information from:
Hidcote Bartrim, nr Chipping
Campden, Gloucestershire
GL55 6LR
Tel: 01386 438333

Nearby sights of interest:
Stanway House; Batsford
Arboretum; Stratford-upon-Avon
(Shakespeare Memorial Theatre,
old city); Ragley Hall.

**Powerful topiary shapes give
strength to the white garden.**

 # *Hidcote Manor*

Location: 6.5km (4 miles) NE of Chipping Campden by B4632

Hidcote is a famous, influential and extremely attractive garden. Its maker Lawrence Johnston was American and a man of means and culture who bought the estate in 1907. It was not a propitious site for a garden, 183m (600ft) up on the top of a wind-blasted hill. There was no garden to speak of but there were some splendid trees, including a lovely group of beeches which Johnston incorporated in his design. He was influenced by the fashion for "architectural" gardens but he devised something that was entirely new, dividing his space into enclosures of strongly varied character and deploying a connoisseur's choice of plants.

Although one of the most visited gardens in England, and much illustrated in books, Hidcote's surprises still have the power to excite. A pair of borders dazzles with Satanic red, ending with two dapper pavilions. Here the mood changes completely; on one side is a green walk, a turf path between giant hedges of hornbeam leading at a great distance to a view of the countryside; straight ahead is the formal hedge on stilts of clipped hornbeam. Closer to the house the atmosphere is sometimes more domestic, cottagey even, with plump topiary and a maze-like pattern of beds. But even here there are startling effects – the swimming pool garden contains a giant raised circle of water almost filling the hedged enclosure that surrounds. Hidcote still presents much for the modern gardener to marvel at.

open: Apr to May, Wed, Thu
and Sun, 2–6pm; Jun to Jul, Wed,
Thu, Sat and Sun, 2–6pm; Aug to
Sep, Wed, Thu and Sun, 2–6pm;
also open Bank Holiday Monday,
2–6pm

Further information from:
Chipping Campden,
Gloucestershire GL55 6LW
Tel and Fax: 01386 438777

Nearby sights of interest:
Stanway House; Batsford
Arboretum; Stratford-upon-Avon
(Shakespeare Memorial Theatre,
old city); Ragley Hall.

Kiftsgate Court

Location: 5km (3 miles) NE of Chipping Campden by B4632

Kiftsgate is next door to Hidcote and they make an exceptionally attractive pair of gardens to visit. Kiftsgate has the better site, on the edge of an escarpment with beautiful views to the Vale of Evesham. The estate was bought in 1917 by Mr and Mrs J B Muir and it was Mrs Muir, known to all plant-lovers as Heather Muir, who inspired the garden. She was among the pioneer rediscoverers of shrub roses and introduced some new varieties of her own. Among these are the celebrated *Rosa filipes* 'Kiftsgate', a lovely rambling rose of irrepressible vigour, and the exquisite *R*. 'Heather Muir', a stately seedling of the Himalayan *R. sericea*. A rose garden enclosed in beech hedges planted almost entirely with old shrub roses is still one of the garden's great features.

Another influence was the tradition of naturalistic planting initiated by one of the great 19th-century gardeners and writers,

William Robinson. On wooded slopes south west of the house Mrs Muir planted Mediterranean-style plants to take advantage of sharp drainage and sunny position. This is not a warm part of the country and it is remarkable what flourishes here – olearias, ceanothus, cistus, phlomis, and many other tender woody plants.

 ## *Melbourne Hall*

Location: 14.5km (9 miles) S of Derby by A453

open: Apr to Sep, Wed, Sat, Sun and Bank Holiday Monday, 2–6pm
open: Aug, daily except first three Mon of the month, 2–5pm

Further information from:
Melbourne, Derbyshire D73 1EN
Tel: 01332 862263
Fax: 01332 862263

Nearby sights of interest:
Calke Abbey; Sudbury Hall; Kedleston Hall.

A rare survival of early 18th-century English formal gardening.

The stone mansion of the Coke family at Melbourne dates back to the 16th century but it was rebuilt in the early 18th century. The great garden craze in England at this time was for layouts influenced by André Le Nôtre. None was on the scale of Versailles and all showed a distinctive Englishness – a playful irregularity often being permitted. Few gardens from this period survive but Melbourne's gardens have scarcely changed since they were laid out by the royal gardener Henry Wise in 1704. Gertrude Jekyll visited the garden in 1903 and wrote of it, "Wise's plan shows how completely the French ideas had been adopted in England, for here again are the handsome pools and fountains, the garden thick-hedged with yew, and the bosquet with its strange paths, green-walled, leading to a large fountain-centred circle in the thicket of the grove." This mysterious formality, which so touched Gertrude Jekyll, is exactly the atmosphere that may be experienced today.

East of the house lawns descend towards a pool, the Great Basin, which is over-looked by an exquisite wrought iron pergola made by Robert Bakewell early in the 18th century. South of this, passing by an immense tunnel of yew dating from the original garden, is a series of lime walks rising to a magnificent lead urn. This, the Four Seasons Monument, is by John van Nost, who was the greatest supplier of garden ornaments in England in the early 18th century. Many other of his works, for which the bills survive in the house's archives, animate the rare historic layout of the garden.

The Menagerie

Location: 8km (5 miles) SE of Northampton off B526

open: Apr to Sep, Thu, 10am–4pm

Further information from:
Horton, Northampton,
Northamptonshire NN7 2BX
Tel: 01604 870957

Nearby sights of interest:
Holdenby House Gardens;
Boughton House.

The Menagerie is a bewitching mid-18th-century building designed by Thomas Wright of Durham, an architect and landscaper little of whose idiosyncratic and delightful work survives. The rare but ruinous Menagerie – built to house a collection of exotic animals – was restored by the late Gervase Jackson-Stops who proceeded to make a garden in keeping with it. It has a most beautiful site on a rise overlooking rolling agricultural landscape.

Pretty borders run along the garden side of the house and there are fields up to the other. There are traces of a formal garden, including a pool which has been restored. Two light-hearted thatched pavilions, one classical, the other Gothic, represent the two faces of 18th-century English taste. An avenue of limes and hornbeam walks provide a gentlemanly setting. The place has a magical air, like the set for a lighthearted opera.

Oxford Botanic Garden

Location: In the centre of Oxford

open: All year, daily except Good Friday and 25 Dec, 9am–5pm (closes 4.30pm in winter)

Further information from:
High Street, Oxford OX1 4AX
Tel: 01865 276920

Nearby sights of interest:
Oxford University buildings;
Ashmolean Museum.

The fine 17th-century entrance to the garden.

Oxford Botanic Garden was established in 1621, the first of its kind in Britain, planted with "diverse simples for the advancement of the faculty of medicine". The magnificent 17th-century gateways were built by Neklaus Stone, a mason associated with Inigo Jones. By the 18th century it had established itself as a centre of botanical research and when Linnaeus visited it in 1721 the garden keeper, John Jacob Dillenius, was so taken with him that he offered him the post of his assistant, which he declined.

The garden today still occupies the same stone-walled site although some of its activities have spilled over into glasshouses and other buildings along the River Cherwell. The study collection is chiefly kept within the walls where much of the garden is laid out in order beds. But there is plenty to interest gardeners as well as botanists here, including the National Collection of Euphorbias. It is also animated by some fine trees. Beyond the walled garden to the south west there is an admirable herbaceous border full of lively planting. Here, too, is a rock garden and a bog garden. The glasshouses contain collections of orchids, tropical lilies, succulents, palms, ferns, and alpines. The place has a buzz of activity and there is much for the gardener to admire and learn from.

Packwood House

Location: 17.5km (11 miles) SE of Birmingham by A34

The gabled house was built in the 16th century but has a largely 17th-century appearance. The site is a flat one, not lending itself to gardening in any special way. The garden makes the most of its site, varying the levels slightly and erupting into the sky with an extraordinary topiary garden. It is concealed behind the house and the first part of the garden is walled in brick with a pretty little yew-hedged sunken flower garden with a narrow pool and herbaceous borders positioned round the hedge. In each corner there is an elegant small 18th-century gazebo. Running along one wall of the garden is a series of beds divided by shaped yew buttresses, planted with an eyestopping combination of roses – bright red 'Lilli Marlene' and lemon yellow 'Bright Smiles'.

At the far end from the house a raised terrace cuts across, with floriferous herbaceous planting above, and stairs leading up to The Multitude. This is a series of monumental upright topiary yew shapes, rounded cones and columns, disposed in front of a mount with a helical box-edged path. This, with its appearance of great antiquity, dates back chiefly to the 19th century, although the mount itself dates from the 1700s. From the top of the mount there is an admirable lofty view of the garden. The topiary itself is a thrilling if slightly sombre sight.

open: Easter to Sep, Wed to Sun and Bank Holiday Monday (closes Good Friday), 1.30–6pm; Oct, Wed to Sun, 12.30–4.30pm

open: Same days, but 2–6pm

Further information from:
Lapworth, Solihull, Warwickshire B94 6AT
Tel: 01564 782024

Nearby sights of interest:
Stratford-upon-Avon (Shakespeare Memorial Theatre, old city); Warwick Castle; Ragley Hall; Hanbury Hall.

Tall, sombre yew shapes – "The Apostles" – lead to a cluster of topiary, "The Multitude".

87

Painswick Rococo Garden

Location: 800m (½ mile) N of Painswick by B4073

open: mid-Jan to Jun, Wed to Sun and Bank Holiday Monday, 11am–5pm; Jul to Aug, daily, 11am–5pm; Sep to Nov, Wed to Sun, 11am–5pm

Further information from:
Painswick, nr Stroud,
Gloucestershire GL6 6TH
Tel: 01452 813204
Fax: 01452 813204

Nearby sights of interest:
Cotswold scenery; Berkeley Castle; Misarden Park Gardens; Gloucester (Cathedral).

Visiting Painswick today it is hard to imagine that in the early 80s the garden was invisible, hidden under a tangle of brambles and saplings. In 1984 the owner Lord Dickinson embarked on an extraordinary private restoration inspired by the survival of a painting by Thomas Robins which appeared to show the garden as it had been in 1748. When the undergrowth was cleared and an archaeological survey carried out, traces of the features shown in Robins's painting were discovered and Lord Dickinson resolved to restore the garden as closely as possible to its state in the mid-18th century.

The garden lies in a secret combe behind the house, hidden in old beech woods through which walks run along the contours giving views of the garden in the valley below. Its layout hovers between formality and a full-blown landscape style, with pretty Gothic buildings forming eye-catchers at the head of an avenue or rearing up on a hill among trees. There is no other surviving garden of this kind, light-heartedly Rococo in spirit.

At the heart of the garden shown in Robins's painting, is an enchanting diamond-shaped formal kitchen garden with a filigree exedra of carved wood at its head. All this has been perfectly reinstated. Today Painswick is not merely a brilliant feat of historical restoration and recreation, but a magical and mysterious garden with an atmosphere like no other.

The Gothic Red House at the end of its avenue.

19 *Plas Brondanw*

Location: 5km (3 miles) N of Penrhyndeudraeth by A4085

In the heart of beautiful countryside, with stunning views of the mountains of Snowdonia, the garden at Plas Brondanw is worthy of its setting. The estate belonged to Clough Williams-Ellis, architect and garden designer, who lived here between 1902 and 1960 creating a garden that is related to its surroundings. It is architectural in spirit, with splendid yew hedges and topiary all taking their cue from the handsome stone house and fixing the garden in its scenery. Peaks of the mountains Snowdon and Cnicht are "borrowed" – one as an eye-catcher exactly aligned with the chief axis of the garden and the other breathtakingly revealed in a "window" cut in a hedge. Everywhere there are lively, often humorous, dashingly executed decorative flourishes.

open: All year, daily, 9am–5pm

Further information from:
Llanfrothen, Penrhyndeudraeth, Gwynned LL48 6SW
Tel: 01766 770 228

Nearby sights of interest:
Scenery of Snowdonia; Portmeirion; Harlech Castle.

20 *Powis Castle*

Location: 1.5km (1 mile) S of Welshpool by A483

The castle has a splendid position, high up on a bluff with immense views overlooking the unspoilt rural landscape. It was built in the 13th century for the ancient Princes of Powys, one of whose descendants sold the estate to the Herberts in the 16th century. Henrietta Herbert married into the Clive family in the 18th century and their descendants still remain at Powis.

The most remarkable thing about the garden is the series of giant 18th-century terraces which descend the slopes below the south-east façade of the castle, balustraded and embellished with beautiful lead statues and urns, from the workshop of the 18th-century Flemish sculpture Jan van Nost. Their planting, in a series of breathtaking mixed borders, is the work first of Graham Stuart Thomas and then of Jimmy Hancock, who retired as head gardener in 1996. The terraces are also ornamented with terracotta pots, placed on the balustrades and niches, showing great imagination in their planting. The north-eastern end of the terraces is closed by ancient hedges of yew and box.

South and east of the castle The Wilderness presents a total change of atmosphere. Here is a fine collection of trees and shrubs built up in the 20th century. Everywhere there are good ornamental trees and shrubs – hollies, hydrangeas, Japanese maples and magnolias, and there is also a superb collection of rhododendrons. This combination of informal woodland planting and the grand formality of the terraces make Powis Castle one of the most attractive and unusual of gardens.

open: Easter to May, Sep to Oct, daily except Mon and Tue, 12 noon to 4pm; Jun to Aug, daily except Mon, 12 noon to 4.30pm. Open every Bank Holiday Monday throughout opening season
open: Same days as garden, 12 noon to 4pm; (closes 4.30pm Jul and Aug)

Further information from:
Welshpool, Powys SY21 8RF
Tel: 01938 554336

Nearby sights of interest:
Stokesay Castle.

The 18th-century terraced garden below the castle.

The Priory

open: Jun to Sep, Fri, 2–6pm

Location: 9.5km (6 miles) S of Pershore by B4080

Further information from:
Kemerton, Gloucestershire
GL20 7JN
Tel: 01386 725258

Nearby sights of interest:
Tewkesbury (Abbey); Stanway House; Sudeley Castle.

Kemerton is a pretty village on the edge of which The Priory has a fine site on the southern slopes of Bredon Hill. The garden is full of decorative features – good ornamental trees, a pergola, fine lawns and much else. But what makes it outstanding is the Top Border – a long, chiefly herbaceous border with beautifully planned colour schemes. At one end it is dominated by silver, pink and white which shifts to yellow and gold. In the middle it explodes into orange, red, and crimson which in turn subside to quiet blue, mauve and white. The whole border, apart from the skilful deployment of colour, also shows contrast of foliage and habit. In the central, fiery section the arching stems of *Rosa* 'Geranium' rise behind the blade-like foliage of crocosmias. Tall kniphofias shoot up from among the palm-shaped leaves of the castor-oil plant (*Ricinus communis*). The bold flowerheads of dahlias jostle with the foliage of ruby chard. It is at its peak in late summer, continuing to give a brilliant display at the end of the opening season. By then seedpods, rosehips and browning top-growth have masked the stronger colours to subtle effect.

Dahlias, heleniums, lavatera, and sedums in a "cool" border.

22 *Renishaw Hall*

Location: 1.5km (1 mile) NW of Junction 30 on the M1

The garden at Renishaw Hall is the remarkable creation of a singular man. In the late 19th century Sir George Sitwell, whose family has lived in these parts for centuries, fell in love with Italian gardens which for years he studied and then decided to distil his knowledge in a new garden for his own house. He was inspired by the Renaissance advice of Leon Battista Alberti who recommended a hillside site for a house with views that "overlook the city, the owner's land, the sea or a great plain and familiar hills and mountains . . . in the foreground there should be a delicacy of gardens".

At the beginning of the 20th century Sitwell embarked on his great work which may be seen today almost exactly as he left it on his death in 1943. It descends in gentle terraces in front of the south façade of the long, grey house. Lawns are hedged in yew which rise in formidable bastions to flank openings. Progressing downwards cross axes reveal enticing views often marked by statues, ornaments or fountains. The hedges are lined with mixed borders, with an exceptional collection of shrub roses, and everywhere the associated planting is of the highest quality. From the bottom terrace, ornamented with a vast scalloped pool and soaring single jet of water, there are huge views over the countryside. This breathtaking but unostentatious scheme is precisely related to the house, following its width exactly. On either side paths lead into woodland where there is a former aviary in the shape of a Gothic temple, countless fine trees and shrubs, an avenue of limes dating back to the 17th century and a colonnaded classical temple in the heart of the woods to the east. All this constitutes a peaceful paradise of the greatest beauty set in an industrial landscape.

open: Easter to mid-Sep, Fri, Sat, Sun and Bank Holiday Monday, 10.30am–4.30pm

Further information from:
Renishaw, Sheffield, Derbyshire
S31 9WB
Tel: 01246 432042

Nearby sights of interest:
Hardwick Hall; Bolsover Castle.

A Derbyshire squire's lovely vision of Renaissance Tuscany.

23

Rousham Park

Location: 19km (12 miles) N of Oxford by A4260 and B4030

open: All year, daily,
10am–4.30pm
open: Apr to Sep, Wed, Sun
and Bank Holiday Monday,
2–4.30pm

Further information from:
Steeple Aston, Oxfordshire
OX6 3QX
Tel: 01869 347110

Nearby sights of interest:
Oxford (University buildings);
Ditchley Park.

Praeneste – William Kent's
arcade of golden stone.

William Kent was a magician of the landscape, the essential
figure in garden history spanning the formality of the early 18th
century with the full-blown informal landscaping of the second
half of the century. Rousham, exquisitely preserved and still in
the hands of the family that commissioned it, is the place to
understand the nature of his genius. The house was built in the
1630s and comprehensively remodelled by Kent 100 years later.
Some of his interiors, in particular the sumptuous but small-scale
Painted Parlour, are among the prettiest rooms of their time.

The garden was laid out early in the 18th century by Charles
Bridgeman, and Kent imposed on that essentially formal layout,
without completely obliterating it, a new kind of garden. Behind
the house a deep, wide lawn reveals sights of the rural landscape
and on one side a path winds down the wooded hill. Below the
path Praeneste, an arcade of honey-coloured stone, has views
down towards the curving River Cherwell and countryside
beyond. In Venus's Vale two pools in a clearing are animated by fine
sculptures – Venus herself balancing on the point of a pediment
over a cascade which is flanked by hissing swans. On one side a
figure of Pan lurks threateningly in the shade of trees and through
the woods a mysterious stone-lined rill winds its way. On the
far side of the house is the Pigeon House Garden, a walled
enclosure about a fine 17th-century dovecote with pretty borders.

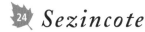

24

Sezincote

Location: 2.5km (1½ miles) W of Moreton-in-Marsh by A44

open: Jan to Nov, Thu, Fri
and Bank Holiday Monday, 2–6pm
open: May to Sep, Thu and
Fri, 2.30–6pm

Further information from:
nr Moreton-in-Marsh,
Gloucestershire GL56 9AW
Tel: 01386 700422

Nearby sights of interest:
Cotswold scenery; Batsford
Arboretum; Stanway House.

The house, of whimsical but refined Indian character, was built
at the beginning of the 19th century by Charles Cockerell. The
family had connections with India, through the East India
Company, and all things Indian were coming into fashion at this
time. The artist Thomas Daniell, who had worked in India,
advised on the garden layout and designed some of the garden
buildings. He was responsible for the delightful bridge, decorated
with cast-iron brahmin bulls which spans the stream to the north
of the house. Below it is a pool with a curious fountain in the form
of a snake entwining a tree-trunk. Upstream from the bridge the
Temple Pool has a Coade-stone figure of Souriya, one of the
three central Vedic deities of the sun, in a stone shrine. The
banks of the pool are planted with cherries, crab apples and more
rarified shrubs like the angelica tree, *Aralia elata* 'Variegata'.

South of the house is a formal Mogul garden designed in the 1960s by the gardener and writer Graham Stuart Thomas. Here, overlooked by the domed house, is an octagonal pool from which two slender canals stretch flanked by Irish yews. To one side is a splendid curving orangery with exquisite Mogul decoration. By some process of alchemy all these exotic ingredients combine to make a peculiarly delicious, and irresistible, scene.

25 *Snowshill Manor*

Location: 5km (3 miles) S of Broadway by minor roads

Snowshill is a Cotswold village of picture-book prettiness and the manor is one of its most attractive houses, dating from the early 16th century with 17th and 18th century additions. The estate was bought in 1919 by Charles Paget Wade, an architect imbued with the philosophy of the Arts and Crafts movement.

Wade contrived a sequence of outdoor rooms on steep slopes to the west of the house. He terraced this area forming a series of courts which, though linked, make the visitor wonder what is coming next. The entrance to the garden follows a path along the southern boundary wall. Here is a pretty border of mallows, hollyhocks, poppies and roses but there is nothing rare or wildly exotic. Plants are not the point at Snowshill, architecture is. An opening pierces the wall and leads into an avenue of Irish yews. The avenue proceeds up a steep path and runs across Armillary Court. Steps lead down to the Well Court with a Venetian well-head frothing with roses and to one side a lily pool. West of this at the lower level is a kitchen garden.

open: Easter to Oct, daily except Tue (closed Good Friday), 12 noon to 5pm; Jul to Aug, also open Tue

open: Same days as garden, 1–5pm

Further information from:
Snowshill, nr Broadway, Gloucestershire WR12 7JU
Tel: 01386 852410

Nearby sights of interest:
Stanway House; Batsford Arboretum; Sudeley Castle.

In Armillary Court, a square lawn with an armillary sphere standing on a tall column with flower beds on two sides.

Stowe Landscape Gardens

Location: 5km (3 miles) NW of Buckingham by A422

open: mid-Apr to beginning of Jul, Mon, Wed, Fri and Sun, 10am–5pm; beginning Jul to beginning Sep, daily, 10am–5pm; beginning Sep to beginning Nov, Mon, Wed, Fri and Sun, 10am–5pm; (also open at other times during school holidays, telephone for details)

open: During school holidays, daily except Sat, 2–5pm

Further information from:
Buckingham, Buckinghamshire
MK18 5EH
Tel: 01280 822850

Nearby sights of interest:
Woburn Abbey; Luton Hoo; Wrest Park.

Stowe is the finest large-scale landscape garden in Britain where, in a single place, it is possible to study and admire almost the whole history of 18th-century landscaping. It has had its ups and downs, including a catastrophic sale in 1922 of the contents of the house and many garden ornaments, but it is remarkable how well the landscape has survived. In addition, Stowe possesses an unequalled collection of 18th-century garden buildings – more than twice as many listed buildings than any other British garden. The house has long been a famous public school, which always recognised the importance of its setting. The landscape with its buildings and ornaments, however, was beyond the means of a school and today the gardens are cared for by the National Trust which has embarked on an ambitious programme of restoration.

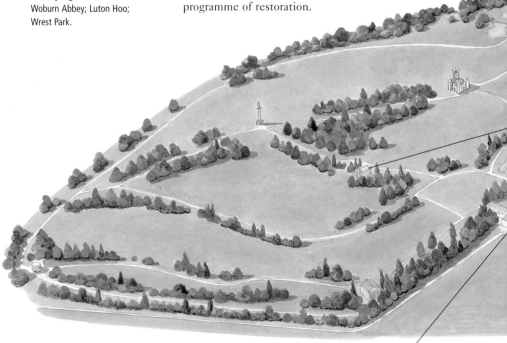

The Grenville Column, a memorial to Thomas Grenville, killed in action in 1747.

The Palladian Bridge, probably designed by James Gibbs and modelled on another at Wilton.

The Queen's Temple (c1754) later renamed after King George III's queen, Charlotte.

The Lake Pavilion, designed by Sir John Vanbrugh between 1714 and 1720.

The Palladian bridge, seen through the Doric Arch (1768) possibly designed by Lord Camelford.

In the 17th century the estate belonged to the Temple family who, early in the following century, started to embellish both house and garden on a grandiose scale. Sir Richard Temple, Viscount Cobham, recruited Charles Bridgeman to lay out a new garden and Sir John Vanbrugh to design garden buildings. The result was a fascinating transitional garden with informal winding walks but also possessing the powerful axial emphasis of earlier formal gardens. William Kent came to Stowe in the 1720s and by the 1730s was laying out a garden in a radically new idiom much of which survives. The Elysian Fields, lying in a shallow valley to one side of the axis of the old formal garden, is a delightful sylvan Arcadia with a winding river and pools. It is overlooked by a domed Temple of Ancient Virtue (William Kent, 1735) raised up on an eminence and originally containing statues of Homer, Socrates, Epaminondas and Lycurgus respectively the greatest poet, philosopher, soldier and law-maker of the ancient world.

On the far bank of the river, facing up towards it is the Temple of British Worthies, a curved gallery of golden stone with niches containing busts of Lord Cobham's heroes bearing inscriptions, probably written by Alexander Pope, describing their virtues. Dating from the same period as Kent's Elysian Field is Hawkwell Field with a remarkable Gothic temple designed in the early 1740s by James Gibbs, and one of the earliest of all buildings in the reborn Gothic style which was soon to become so fashionable. This was originally a *ferme ornée* with a hayfield at its centre and it preserves an agricultural flavour with sheep round about. South of it, at the foot of the slope, is a Palladian Bridge copied from the Italian architect Palladio's design. It has a charming setting, spanning a river with cattle grazing in pastures, and clumps and belts of trees along the river banks. Half concealed in the trees, overlooking the river, is a little pavilion with a curved seat above which the wall is prettily decorated in pebble work with the arms of the Temple family and their punning motto: *Templa quam dilecta* ("how beautiful are your temples"). Along the river there is a pair of classical buildings, the Lake Pavilions. From this point there is a view back towards the house at the end of a vista which was established by Bridgeman's layout almost 300 years ago. Its effect is now softened but it plainly shows how strongly a formal feature may survive in an informal 18th-century landscape park.

In 1741 "Capability" Brown, then only 25, was appointed head gardener at Stowe. In 1747 he laid out the Grecian Valley, north of Hawkwell Field, using already the characteristic Brownian ingredients of shorn turf and subtly undulating belts of trees. Tucked away to one side is the Temple of Concord, completed long after Brown had left Stowe. It was started by Kent, and finished by G B Borra in 1764 to celebrate the end of the Seven Years War the previous year.

The Oxford Bridge (1761) includes parts of an earlier temple designed by Sir John Vanbrugh.

There are a number of other buildings to admire, all deftly fitted into vistas, glades, walks and eminences. The trees are marvellous, too, including magnificent cedars of Lebanon. Trees have to be spectacular to make an impact in the context of this giant landscape and its spectacular monuments.

The 18th-century poet James Thomson wrote, "Oh! lead me to the wide extended walks,/The fair majestic paradise of Stowe!". Modern visitors will also enjoy wide extended walks, animated by some of the loveliest buildings in the country. For those less mobile, electric buggies may be hired at the entrance. There are 101ha (250 acres) of the park to visit and it is best to think of it as a whole day's excursion, perhaps punctuated by a picnic lunch taken in the grandest surroundings.

William Kent's Temple of Ancient Virtue (1736) overlooking the Elysian Fields.

Tatton Park

Location: 5.5km (3½ miles) N of Knutsford

open: Apr to Sep, daily
except Mon (open every Bank
Holiday Monday), 10.30am–6pm;
Oct to Mar, daily except Mon,
11am–4pm

open: Same months, Tue to
Sun, 12 noon to 4pm

Further information from:
Knutsford, Cheshire WA16 6QN
Tel: 01565 654822
Fax: 01565 650179

Nearby sights of interest:
Dunham Massey.

The Egertons have lived in these parts since the 16th century. A new house was built to the designs of Samuel Wyatt from 1788 onwards, completed by his nephew Lewis Wyatt early in the next century but the garden history of Tatton Park goes back much further.

Visitors approach the garden across a magnificent former deer park and an avenue of beeches, planted in 1737, many still surviving, which once marked the chief approach to the house. The periods of greatest garden activity were in the 19th and 20th centuries. Lewis Wyatt designed a fine orangery on the southern corner of the house and a little later, in 1859, Joseph Paxton created a magnificent fernery – both these survive. Paxton was also responsible for the Italian Garden to the south-east of the house, an elaborate parterre of bedding schemes laid out about the Italianate Neptune Fountain. The Broad Walk, ending in a copy of the Athenian Choragic Monument of Lysicrates, running north-west/south-east, forms the chief axis of the garden. It follows the original entrance to the house and is still lined by a beech avenue going back to the early 18th century. At its beginning are mixed borders – the "L-borders" backed by walls originally heated to provide early or tender fruit. Further from the house the garden assumes a woodland character, with many good trees and shrubs. Among a series of lakes is a Japanese garden made by Japanese craftsman in 1910 for the third Lord Egerton. Spreading Japanese Maples, azaleas, water irises, a tea-house and snow lanterns form a delightful evocation of the Japanese spirit. Such gardens are wildly inauthentic but evince great admiration for Japanese culture which became immensely fashionable at the turn of the century.

The Japanese garden (1910) with thatched tea-house, Japanese maples, and brilliant azaleas.

You will leave the garden is by a route which was planned by Humphry Repton in the early 19th century as the new approach to the house. Looking back it is possible to judge how successful Repton was in his desire to make "the approach convenient, interesting, and in strict harmony with the Character and Situation of the mansion to which it must point the way".

28 *Tretower Court*

Location: 5km (3 miles) NW of Crickhowell by A479

The delightful house of Tretower Court dates from the 15th century when it was built for Sir Roger Vaughan. It has been finely restored and, although unfurnished, is particularly worth visiting if only to admire the charming views of the garden below. The garden is a reconstruction, made in 1991, of the sort of a garden a house of this kind might have had in the Middle Ages.

The entrance passes through a cobbled yard and immediately leads into a tunnel arbour festooned with grapevines, honeysuckle and roses such as *Rosa* x *alba* 'Alba Semiplena', a garden rose of immense antiquity. A herber fenced in trelliswork has raised flower beds planted with many herbs. On the other side of the path another enclosure has a fountain and a series of chequerboard beds planted with daisies, lilies, peonies, primulas and violas – all species known in gardens before 1500. Across a flowery meadow there is a group of cider apple trees – not ancient varieties, for none survive from the Middle Ages. All this is charmingly done and it is hard to think of any better way of complementing the exceptional buildings of the Court.

open: Easter to Oct, daily, 9.30am–6pm
open: As above

Further information from:
Tretower, nr Crickhowell,
Powys NP8 1RF
Tel: 01874 730279

Nearby sights of interest:
The Brecon Beacons.

A recreated Medieval pool and fountain in the flower garden.

---

29 *Waddesdon Manor*

Location: 9.5km (6 miles) NW of Aylesbury by A41

This part of Buckinghamshire was dominated by the Rothschild family and Waddesdon Manor was one of their finest flings. Baron Ferdinand de Rothschild bought the estate in 1874 and his house, built to the designs of Hippolyte Destailleur, was finished in 1880. There is nothing like it in Britain, a richly romantic vision of a château of the Renaissance. Destailleur incorporated into the house superb French rooms, dating from the 17th and 18th centuries, many of which were rescued from houses destroyed during Haussmann's refashioning of Paris in the 1860s.

A Frenchman, Elie Lainé, was commissioned to lay out the grounds, planting windbreaks and planning winding drives and walks. Countless trees and shrubs were planted on the slopes below the house which were enlivened by Baron Ferdinand's collection of statues and urns, most of which are still in place. In recent years the house and garden have been finely restored, including a dazzling parterre now replanted with bedding plants evoking the splendours of high Victorian garden style. No-one should visit the gardens without also seeing the house whose rooms are full of the finest furniture, china and paintings.

open: Mar to mid-Dec, Wed to Sun and Bank Holiday Monday, 10am–5pm
open: Easter to Oct, Thu to Sun and Bank Holiday Monday, plus Wed in Jul and Aug, 11am–4pm

Further information from:
Waddesdon, nr Aylesbury,
Buckinghamshire HP18 0JH
Tel: 01296 651211

Nearby sights of interest:
Oxford (University buildings, Botanic Garden, Ashmolean Museum).

30 *Westbury Court Garden*

Location: 14.5km (9 miles) SW of Gloucester by A48

open: Easter to Oct, Wed to Sun and Bank Holiday Monday (closes Good Friday), 11am–6pm

Further information from:
Westbury-on-Severn,
Gloucestershire GL14 1PD
Tel: 01452 760461

Nearby sights of interest:
Gloucester (Cathedral); Misarden Park; scenery of the Wye Valley.

Westbury Court Garden is a rare and lovely survivor. In this watery part of England there was in the 17th century a strong tradition of gardens, probably influenced by Dutch examples, in which formal water features played an important part. Westbury has only just survived, for the house to which it belonged has long since disappeared and the garden itself lay derelict for years. The garden was started in 1697 by Maynard Colchester whose family remained here for almost 300 years, the estate finally being sold to a developer in 1960. In 1967 the National Trust undertook a pioneer restoration, greatly helped by the survival in the County Record Office of Colchester's account books with meticulous records of plants bought – "Pd Mr Wells 12 spruce firrs 24 Scotch firrs £1:2:0".

The garden is enclosed in walls of old bricks and two parallel canals run almost its whole length. One is edged with yew hedges which are ornamented at the top with lollipops and finials of clipped holly. At its head is a tall, pillared, pedimented summerhouse of strikingly Dutch appearance. In one corner of the garden is a secret garden with a pretty brick summerhouse. The walls are planted with old varieties of espaliered fruit and period cultivars of garden plants are used, but not exclusively, in borders. At the northern end of the garden the wall is pierced by a *claire-voyée* with beautiful early 18th-century railings flanked by stone piers with handsomely carved urns.

The parterre faithfully recreated from a contemporary engraving and using period plants.

31 *Westonbirt Arboretum*

Location: 5km (3 miles) SW of Tetbury by A433

open: All year, daily,
10am–8pm (or sunset, if earlier)

Further information from:
Westonbirt, nr Tetbury,
Gloucestershire GL8 8QS
Tel: 01666 880220
Fax: 01666 880559

Nearby sights of interest:
Bath (Abbey, Georgian
architecture); Cotswold scenery;
Rodmarton Manor Gardens.

Japanese maples in autumn.

This is one of the greatest collections of woody plants in Europe. Unlike most plant collections it has the charm of being a most attractive piece of landscaping in which the plants are arranged with great skill. It was started by Robert Holford in 1829 and was developed by the Holford family well into the present century.

Holford planted windbreaks and then major avenues to divide up the space, grouping trees in dramatic clumps, placing individual specimens in positions of prominence to lure the visitor on. Trees planted by him still survive – among them superb incense cedars (*Calocedrus decurrens*) and Wellingtonias (*Sequoiadendron giganteum*). He also grouped trees and shrubs with fine autumn foliage – the Colour Circle of plants such as Japanese maples, *Liquidambar styraciflua*, and *Parrotia persica*. A National Collection of Japanese maples is now held at Westonbirt. Apart from the trees there is an immense range of ornamental shrubs – eucryphias, pieris, rhododendrons, stuartias, and many more. It is inconceivable that any gardener could come here and not find something to marvel at. There are over 3,000 plants to be seen in an area of over 243ha (600 acres).

32 *Wollerton Old Hall*

Location: 2.5km (1½ miles) NE of Hodnet by A53

open: Jun to Aug, Fri and
Sun, 12 noon to 5pm

Further information from:
Wollerton, Market Drayton,
Shropshire TF9 3NA
Tel: 01630 685756
Fax: 01630 685583

Nearby sights of interest:
Hodnet Hall; Hawkstone Park.

It is reassuring to know that new gardens of real quality are still being made. This was started in 1984 and is now one of the liveliest and most attractive in the country. Although it does nothing new – it is in the tradition of gardens of enclosures – it is carried off with rare skill and connoisseurship of plants.

An underlying grid of paths and axes unites the ingredients giving harmony to the whole. At the heart of it is a sunken garden with narrow rill running from a pool, aligned with a long pergola. At right angles a border runs along a wall and a path leads to a white garden. In contrast to it is the neighbouring enclosure in which brilliantly coloured plants are intermingled. Beyond it an openwork gazebo lies at the centre of burgeoning borders and there is a hidden kitchen garden. The way back to the entrance is along a serene walk of magnolias, Japanese maples and other shrubs. The garden is beautifully kept and everywhere there are well judged arrangements of plants.

Key to gardens

1	Belsay Hall	6	Herterton House Gardens	11	Newby Hall Gardens
2	Bramham Park	7	Holker Hall	12	Seaton Delaval Hall
3	Castle Howard	8	Howick Hall	13	Studley Royal
4	Cragside House	9	Levens Hall	14	Wallington
5	Duncombe Park	10	Muncaster Castle		

Key

- ═══ Motorways
- ═══ Principal trunk highways
- ③ Gardens
- ● Major towns and cities
- • Towns

Garden tours

- Northern tour: 12, 1, 6, 14, 4,
- Central tour: 2, 11, 13, 5, 3

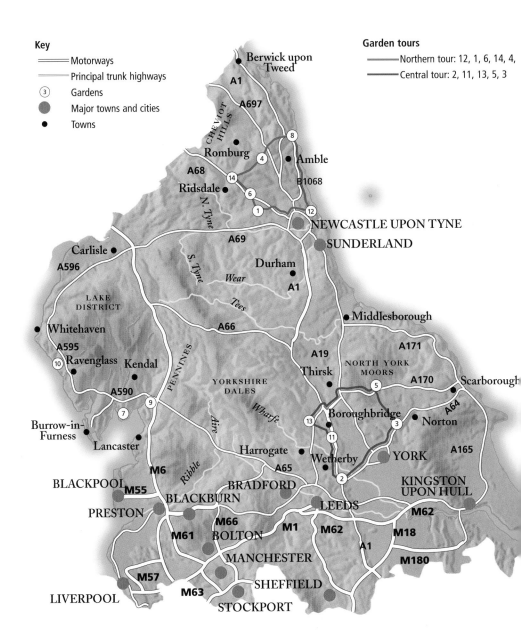

North
England

We find the same broad differences of climate here as are to be found elsewhere in England, with relatively high rainfall to the west and a much drier climate to the east. In the northern part of the region the Pennines form a natural dividing barrier. The climate here is very harsh and no notable gardens are to be found, although there are distinguished nurseries some of which, capitalizing on their position, specialize in alpine plants.

Garden taste in Britain often tends to be influenced by what is fashionable in London and the south. Here, far from such influences, there is an independence of ideas that has resulted in gardens strikingly different from those in other parts of the country. Several of the gardens included in this section belong to great estates,

many of which have had astonishing continuity of ownership. Castle Howard and Bramham Park both remain in the ownership of the families that built them. But this by no means implies conservatism in garden taste. Both have gardens of stiking originality executed on the grand scale.

A low terraced walk runs along one side of the walled garden in Wallington.

Castle Howard (p.107) in North Yorkshire is a wonderful example of the ways in which northern gardens are quite different from others. On this exposed and wildly romantic stretch of moorland Sir John Vanbrugh, the English Baroque architect and dramatist, devised a marvellously theatrical landscape – open, blasted by winds and on a heroic scale making even the largest southern landscape gardens seem tame. The early 18th-century Bramham Park (see p.106), also in Yorkshire, is unique in a different way. Although it is vast, the radiating avenues of ancient beech hedges and its less flamboyant garden buildings than those of Castle Howard give an almost intimate atmosphere. The region is rich in 18th-century gardens of many kinds – the valley garden of Studley Royal (see p.115), the beautiful terraces and temples of Duncombe Park (see p.109), and the mist-shrouded splendours of Seaton Delaval Hall (see p.114). Studley Royal and Duncombe Park, although physically far removed from metropolitan taste, both capitalized on their unique settings to make a revolutionary type of landscape. Studley Royal was started in the 1720s and as the century moved on the garden changed to suit the mood of the time. Crisp Baroque formality in the early part of the period became Picturesque naturalism by the 1760s when the ruins of Fountains Abbey were woven into the garden scheme. At Duncombe Park a giant terrace was built in the 1730s to take advantage of the beautiful views of the River Rye.

There are many fine 20th-century gardens, such as Newby Hall (see p.113) with its dazzling borders and rare plants, and Holker Hall (see p.111) with its lively, decorative spirit. Lastly, the most beautiful flower garden in the region – Herterton House Gardens (see p.110) in Northumberland, created since 1975, is a feast of brilliant colours and subtle design.

The flower garden at Herterton House Gardens.

open: Apr to Oct, daily, 10am–6pm (closes 4pm Nov to Mar); closes 25 and 26 Dec, 1 Jan
open: As above

Further information from:
Belsay, near Newcastle-upon-Tyne, Northumberland NE20 0DX
Tel: 01661 881636
Fax: 01661 881043

Nearby sights of interest:
Hadrian's Wall; Hexham Abbey.

Rhododendrons in the wild and picturesque quarry garden.

Belsay Hall

Location: 22.5km (14 miles) NW of Newcastle by A696

Sir Charles Monck (who changed his name to Middleton) came back from an extended honeymoon in Greece determined to build something at Belsay inspired by his study of the Classical world. His Greek Revival mansion was built between 1810 and 1817, of the curious red-brown stone quarried on the site. The resulting workings were transformed into a dramatic quarry garden inspired by the theories of the picturesque, which were so fashionable at the turn of the 18th century. Between rocky crags he made a path which meandered steeply uphill to the 14th-century Belsay Castle. This ravine provided the setting for naturalistic planting – flowering shrubs, shade-loving plants, wild roses, spectacular *Cardiocrinum giganteum*, and rare honeysuckles tumbling down the rocks. Closer to the house there is formal planting – a circular bed, for example, of *Crambe cordifolia* under-planted with *Allium cristophii*, and white annual mallows, all hedged in lavender. From a terrace there are glimpses across a field of a splendid pinetum, with trees erupting from ramparts of old rhododendrons. Unfortunately, this is no longer part of the estate and not open to the public. The rare quarry garden, however, makes Belsay a marvellous place to visit.

open: end Jun to beginning Sep (open Easter weekend, spring Bank Holiday weekend), Sun, Tue, Wed, Thu, 1.15–5.30pm
open: As above

Further information from:
Wetherby, West Yorkshire LS23 6ND
Tel: 01937 844265
Fax: 01937 845923

Nearby sights of interest:
Harewood House; Temple Newsam; York (Minster and old city).

Bramham Park

Location: 8km (5 miles) S of Wetherby by A1

Bramham Park is an exceptionally attractive 18th-century formal garden. The stone house was built in 1698 for Robert Benson, the first Lord Bingley, who had recently completed his Grand Tour. For the design of his house he drew on Italian ideas, and for his garden on the formal gardens of France – in both cases it seems likely that he himself was the designer.

Below the west façade of the house lies a formal rose garden. All is symmetrical here, with a regular pattern of bedding roses and an avenue of yews clipped into columns. Beyond this is a giant formal park – 40ha (100 acres) of walks and rides, often hedged in beech which rises in many places to a height of 8m (25ft). Near the house a chapel marks the beginning of an immense axis running south-east. It passes by a huge formal pool, continuing to a domed rotunda. The vista continues to a soaring obelisk, also at the centre of a pattern of paths, and beyond that to the countryside. This is a place for a long walk on a bright and windy day, with beautiful things to see at every turn.

Castle Howard

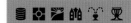

Location: 22.5km (14 miles) NE of York by A64

"I never was so agreeably astonished in my days, as with the first vision of the whole place . . . I have seen gigantic places before, but never a sublime one" wrote Horace Walpole, that eagle-eyed connoisseur of houses and gardens, in the mid-18th century. The house was built, starting on a virgin site in 1700, for Lord Carlisle by Sir John Vanbrugh, an astonishing first venture for the novice architect. The gigantic Baroque house was designed on a scale dramatic enough to hold its own in this wild part of the Yorkshire moors. Vanbrugh was also involved in the layout of the garden – an early 18th-century engraving illustrates a theatrical formal wilderness south of the house.

Today, although there are pretty formal gardens near the house – a walled rose garden and the splendid remains of W A Nesfield's Victorian water parterre – the essential thing about Castle Howard is the giant landscape embellished with magnificent buildings. South east of the castle the New River flows into two formal pools linked by cascades. The Prince of Wales Fountain in the South Lake has a giant single jet encircled by a series of minor jets. Above the lake are two exceptional park buildings. The Temple of the Four Winds (Vanbrugh, 1724–8) has an elaborate dome and columned pediments on each of its façades. The massive Mausoleum to the south east (Nicholas Hawksmoor, 1726–9) is in the form of a rotunda, walled in columns, and rising no less than 27m (90ft) high among the sheep grazing peacefully around. These monuments are relatively close to the castle but many others animate the larger landscape, including a huge obelisk (1714) at the junction of two giant vistas. Immediately east of the castle is Ray Wood, part of the formal garden scheme in the early 18th century. Since World War II it has been transformed into an exceptional woodland garden with countless trees and shrubs, fastidiously chosen by the late James Russell.

open: Mid-Mar to beginning Nov, daily, 10am–5pm (also partly open in winter, telephone for details)
open: Same days, 11am–5pm

Further information from:
nr York, North Yorkshire YO6 7DA
Tel: 01653 648444
Fax: 01653 648462

Nearby sights of interest:
Rievaulx Abbey.

The south of the castle: W A Nesfield's formal garden of the 1850s with the Atlas Fountain.

open: Easter to Oct, Tue to Sun (open Bank Holiday Monday), 10.30am–6.30pm; Nov to mid-Dec, Sat, Sun and Tue, 10.30am–4pm
open: Same days, 1–5.30pm

Further information from:
Rothbury, Morpeth,
Northumberland NE65 7PX
Tel: 01669 20333

Nearby sights of interest:
Alnwick Castle; Bamburgh Castle.

Cragside House

Location: 21km (13 miles) SW of Alnwick by B6341

This is a wild part of the country and the house at Cragside is a match for it in every way. The very name gives an idea of the effect the architect, Norman Shaw, wanted to achieve. It was built in 1870 on a site where no house had previously existed, for the armaments tycoon, the first Lord Armstrong. The site is appropriately dramatic, on a rocky cliff rising above Debdon Burn.

There are two gardens at Cragside, lying on either side of the valley. Immediately below the house a spectacular rock garden tumbles down towards the stream, looking more like an eruption of nature than the work of man. This is richly planted with alpine flowers, and wilder, more substantial trees and shrubs, among them berberis, wild roses and rowans. The rockery extends down to the valley bottom where a fine pinetum runs along the banks of the stream. At this point there is a bridge and a climb up the facing slopes towards the second garden. This is then a stiffish walk but an exceptionally attractive one. The goal is a formal garden set about glasshouses of the same date as the house. The Orchard House has an extraordinary series of little turntables with fruit in pots sitting on them, which gently rotate so that all fruit is equally exposed to the light. The power for these is hydraulic, for Lord Armstrong was devoted to the latest machinery. Cragside was the first house in the world to be lit by electricity which was generated by hydraulic power. Beside the glasshouse, arranged on sloping beds, is a virtuoso display of Victorian carpet bedding and behind it tropical and temperate ferneries can be found.

Carpet bedding and the Gothic estate clock in the glasshouse yard.

Duncombe Park

Location: 9km (12 miles) E of Thirsk by A170

open: Good Friday to beginning of Nov, Sat to Wed, 11am–6pm; May to Sep, daily, 11am–6pm
open: As above

Further information from:
Helmsley, North Yorkshire YO6 5EB
Tel: 01439 770213
Fax: 01439 771114

Nearby sights of interest:
Rievaulx Abbey.

In the 18th century the landscape itself became an object of interest to connoisseurs. If a garden was fortunate enough to command some splendid prospect this was often made into the focal point of a designed park. The house at Duncombe was built in the very early 18th century to the designs of William Wakefield in the theatrically Baroque style of Sir John Vanbrugh and he quite possibly was also involved in its design. The owner of the estate was Thomas Duncombe who took a keen interest in landscape design.

Duncombe Park has a magnificent site, on the edge of an escarpment with beautiful views over the wooded banks of the River Rye and the rooftops of the ancient town of Helmsley with its ruined castle. Immediately to the east of the house a curved terrace was constructed some time before 1730 to take advantage of the view. At both ends of the house there is a striking building: to the north an Ionic temple and to the south a Doric temple with a dome, girdled with columns. The Doric temple is raised on a mound and has especially fine views, including those of a picturesque cascade in the river below which was certainly part of the 18th-century designed landscape. From the Doric temple a shorter, and perfectly straight, terrace leads due west with, halfway along, a 19th-century conservatory partly concealed in a clearing in the woods. Although there are other attractions at Duncombe, including marvellous trees and some pretty Victorian parterres, the most memorable attraction is the extraordinary terrace and the Elysian views disclosed from its heights.

The Doric Temple, built in the 1730s by an unknown architect, on the terrace.

Herterton House Gardens

Location: 3km (2 miles) N of Cambo by B6342

open: Apr to Sep, daily except Tue and Thu, 1.30–5.30pm

Further information from:
Hartington, nr Cambo,
Northumberland NE61 6BN
Tel: 01670 774278

Nearby sights of interest:
Hadrian's Wall; Hexham Abbey;
Wallington Hall.

This is a unique and remarkable garden. The owners are artists who have made their garden their medium. Taking advantage of the architectural setting, an ancient stone farmhouse and its finely built outhouses and walls, they have assembled an astonishing range of plants disposed with the greatest skill.

The largest part of the garden is the walled flower garden. An underlying grid of beds and paths, arranged to a modular base like a painting by the abstract artist Mondrian, presents a lavish patchwork of colour and form. The colours are carefully arranged with cooler yellows and blues near the house, becoming hotter – reds, oranges, and purples – as the garden extends away from the house. Much of the planting is herbaceous, usually species plants or natural forms, and often of English natives. They derive harmony from restricted colour groupings and from the underlying grid of beds. Within the beds the plants are not grouped in swathes in Jekyllian style, but used individually to provide notes of colour or shapely outlines.

Much use is made of different species of box to provide a structure of permanent shapes and hedges. At the centre of the physic garden lies an immense drum of clipped silver pear (*Pyrus salicifolia* 'Pendula') about which is arranged a parterre of herbal, medicinal or otherwise useful plants. To the front of the house a strip of garden along the road has strong shapes of box hedging and topiary with emphatic underplanting of different species of dicentra. The whole garden has a magical air and its appearance will stick in the visitor's mind with extraordinary tenacity.

Herbaceous planting in the flower garden with fastidious colour schemes.

Holker Hall

Location: 6.5km (4 miles) W of Grange-over-Sands

open: Apr to Oct, daily
except Sat, 10.30am–6pm
open: As above

Further information from:
Cark-in-Cartmel, nr Grange-over-
Sands, Cumbria LA11 7PL
Tel: 01539 558328
Fax: 01539 558776

Nearby sights of interest:
Lake District.

The present appearance of the house at Holker, built of pale pink stone in a romantic neo-Jacobean style, dates from the 1870s, when it was completely rebuilt after two fires. The history of the estate is an ancient one, going back to the Middle Ages when it was part of Cartmel Priory. Although there are traces of an older garden here, Holker Hall owes most of its horticultural distinction to the 19th and 20th centuries. There was a formal garden here in the early 18th century but all signs of it were removed when the gardens were landscaped later in the century. A few splendid specimens of trees survive from this time.

The Cavendishes of Chatsworth lived here in the 19th century (and still do) and did much to the garden under the influence of Sir Joseph Paxton, the head gardener at Chatsworth (see p.81). From this period shrubs and trees – especially conifers – still survive. The climate here is remarkably mild, the soil is acid and the rainfall exceptionally high. These conditions are especially favourable for rhododendrons, which were planted in quantity in the later 19th century, and for countless other distinguished shrubs which continue to be planted. Today not only are the gardens beautifully kept, but there is a lively decorative sense particularly visible in the borders about the house.

Crocosmia and *Macleaya cordata* ornament the formal garden.

Howick Hall

Location: 9.5km (6 miles) NE of Alnwick by B1340 and minor roads

open: Apr to Oct, daily,
1–6pm

Further information from:
Alnwick, Northumberland
NE66 3LB
Tel and Fax: 01665 577285

Nearby sights of interest:
Alnwick Castle; Bamburgh Castle;
Farne Islands; Lindisfarne.

Howick Hall lies quite close to the sea and enjoys a mild microclimate. Most of the soil is alkaline but, at a little distance from the house, a rich acid seam in a protected low-lying position allows the cultivation of ericaceous shrubs. The woodland garden created here between World War I and II benefited directly from the flood of new plant discoveries made by George Forrest and Frank Kingdon Ward, chiefly in the Himalayas. Seed from these expeditions made its way to Howick and resulted in a marvellous collection of rhododendrons, camellias and magnolias. These are richly underplanted with such herbaceous plants as hostas, lilies, the brilliant blue Himalayan poppy, orchids, and species peonies. Close to the house sun-loving plants such as agapanthus and kniphofias flourish in alkaline soil and further away excellent small trees, including such maples as *Acer saccharum* and *A. griseum*, are planted in rough grass. The gardens at Howick preserve an air of seclusion and privacy.

111

🛢 🍽 🌸 ⚘

🌿 **open:** Apr to Sep, daily
except Fri and Sat, 11am–5pm
⛪ **open:** As above

Further information from:
Kendall, Cumbria LA8 0PD
Tel: 01539 560321
Fax: 01539 560669

Nearby sights of interest:
Lake District; Sizergh Castle.

 Levens Hall

Location: 8km (5 miles) S of Kendal by A591

A writer in the magazine *Country Life* in 1899 was amazed by what he saw at Levens Hall: "Fantastic forms rise in yew, strange and remarkable, as far as the eye can reach – a peacock here, a huge umbrella-like construction there, an archway, a lion . . . . A bewildering world of gardening, some may say!" The same extraordinary shapes of yew topiary are in the garden today and still impart a surreal air of mystery.

The garden was laid out towards the end of the 17th century by a Frenchman, Guillaume Beaumont, about whose work almost nothing is known. A portrait of him, still hanging at the house, is inscribed with the words "he laid out the gardens at Hampton Court Palace and at Levens" but there is no evidence of his having worked at Hampton Court. There is no doubt, though, that he made the garden for Colonel James Grahme at Levens, much of whose original plan still survives. The yew garden to the east of the house has a few specimens which could date from the original plantings but most date from the 19th and 20th centuries.

Their delightful shapes are disposed in a pattern of box-edged beds which are planted with lively bedding schemes for spring and summer. These brilliant blocks of colour make a fine contrast to the sombre yew. Also dating from Beaumont's time is a spectacular walk of beech hedges, now over 300 years old, forming a north-south axis extending from the house. At its centre it opens out into a spacious rondel and the hedges themselves have grown so broad that it is possible to walk among the ancient gnarled branches at their interior. The garden, still privately owned, is beautifully maintained. The house with its great defensive pele tower dating from the 13th century is also worth visiting if only to see the portrait of Monsieur Beaumont and a fascinating plan of the garden dating from 1730. Today's garden is astonishingly close to that plan.

Powerful topiary shapes complement the Medieval fortified house.

Muncaster Castle

Location: 1.5km (1 mile) SE of Ravenglass by A595

Muncaster Castle overlooks the three-fingered estuary of the River Esk on one side and Eskdale, one of the most beautiful valleys of the Lake District, on the other. The first castle was built here in the 13th century and a great deal was added and changed in later periods. In the 1860s it was rebuilt for Lord Muncaster by the architect Anthony Salvin who made a speciality of such things. Lord Muncaster planted many parkland trees in the 1780s some of which survive, including beautiful old sweet chestnuts. Between World Wars I and II Sir John Ramsden built up a collection of rhododendrons which flourish in the mild, wet climate and acid soil. He also experimented with hybridization and the results are a great feature of the gardens. Running along the contours of the slope to one side of the castle is an 18th-century terraced walk, edged with hummocks of yew and box, with views of Eskdale and Sca Fell.

open: All year, daily, 11am–5pm

open: Easter to Oct, daily except Mon, 1–4pm

Further information from:
Ravenglass, Cumbria CA18 1RQ
Tel: 01229 717614
Fax: 01229 717010

Nearby sights of interest:
Lake District.

 # *Newby Hall Gardens*

Location: 6.5km (4 miles) SE of Ripon by B6265

Newby Hall is one of the most beautiful houses in England set in gardens that are entirely worthy of it. The house, of faded brick and stone, dates from the late 17th century but was added to, with some exquisite interiors, by Robert Adam in the 1760s. There was a distinguished garden here in the late 17th century which Daniel Defoe described in 1720 – "the gardens are not only well laid out, but well planted, and as well kept; the statues are neat, the parterres beautiful." Traces of this formal garden are still to be seen: of a lime avenue for example, but for the most part the garden dates from the 20th century.

South of the house formality reigns, with a lily pond and a splendid cross axis of a statue walk with a broad grass path with rows of Irish yews and fine statues. To one side is a sunken garden enclosed in yew hedges. At right angles to the statue walk, forming the north-south axis of the garden, is a spectacular pair of herbaceous borders which run all the way down to the banks of the River Ure. On either side of the borders are less formal parts of the garden in which there are marvellous trees and shrubs. Of special interest is the National Collection of dogwoods (*Cornus* spp.) – well over 80 species, hybrids and cultivars.

open: Easter to Sep, daily (closes Mon except Bank Holiday Monday), 11am–5.30pm

open: As above

Further information from:
Ripon, North Yorkshire HG4 5AE
Tel: 01423 322583
Fax: 01423 324452

Nearby sights of interest:
Fountains Abbey; Studley Royal; Thorp Perrow Arboretum; York (Minster and old city).

The south of the house, from the double herbaceous borders.

Seaton Delaval Hall

Location: 13.5km (9 miles) NE of Newcastle-upon-Tyne on the A190

open: May to Sep, Wed, Sun and Bank Holiday Monday, 2–6pm

Further information from:
Seaton Delaval, Whitley Bay, Northumberland NE26 4QR
Tel: 01912 370786

Nearby sights of interest:
Marsden Rock.

The formal garden designed by James Russell.

The extraordinary house at Seaton Delaval was built in the 1720s by Sir John Vanbrugh for a naval officer, Admiral George Delaval, within splashing distance of the waves of Whitley Bay. Although the surroundings have been harmed by industrial and suburban development it is still a dramatic site and a scarcely less dramatic house, its stone elevations soaring upwards in Baroque flourishes. The house was twice struck by fire – the second time, in 1822, gutting the central part of the house which has never been inhabited since. There are signs that Vanbrugh had a hand in the gardens: to the west of the house there are traces of his characteristic earthworks, providing viewing platforms over what was then encircling countryside. His thoroughly theatrical house may be thought of as a giant ornament of the landscape.

Almost all of the garden seen by visitors today has been made since World War II. Its gentle formality makes an admirable foil for the exuberant house. To the west of the house, entered by a pair of superb wrought-iron gates of the same date as the house, is a refined formal garden designed by James Russell. On either side a series of circles of clipped box encloses mounds of clipped santolina with urns rising in alternate circles. The whole is backed by processions of yew shapes formed into "sentry boxes". At the centre is a fountain and a figure of Diana, the Roman goddess of hunting. overlooks the scene. By the south-west corner of the house, also designed by James Russell, is a rose parterre – a series of geometric box-edged beds brimming with bedding roses. There are fine 18th-century statues in the garden – among them, overlooking the rose parterre at its western end, a dramatic lead cast of Samson slaying a Philistine.

13 *Studley Royal*

Location: 6.5km (4 miles) W of Ripon by B6265

The garden at Studley Royal was created by a father and son, John and Robert Aislabie. The father was Chancellor of the Exchequer at the time of the South Sea Bubble, the great financial collapse in 1722. After imprisonment in the Tower of London he retired to his Yorkshire estate to cultivate his garden. On an extraordinary beautiful site in the rocky, wooded Skelldale, he contrived an immense semi-formal water garden animated by ornaments and buildings. His son Robert continued the garden after his father's death in 1744, by which time the influence of the new landscape style was beginning to be felt. Robert acquired the exquisite ruins of the Cistercian Fountains Abbey in 1768, deftly introducing it into the designed landscape as a stunning eye-catcher. The sides of the valley are laced with walks which are decorated with fine 18th-century garden buildings – including a seat placed so as to give a lofty view of the abbey. From the Octagon Tower there are beautiful views over John Aislabie's water garden – a long, thin canal and a circular pool flanked by triangular pools. On the wooded heights on the far side of the valley the Palladian Banqueting House can be glimpsed, built in the 1730s probably to the designs of Colen Campbell. These and other buildings are carefully placed either to command a carefully orchestrated view, or to ornament some promontory – sometimes both.

開 open: Apr to Sep, daily, 10am–7pm; Oct to Mar, daily, 10am–5pm (or dusk, if earlier); Nov to Jan, Sat to Thu, 10–5pm (or dusk, if earlier); closes 24 and 25 Dec

Further information from:
Fountains, Ripon, North Yorkshire
HG4 3DZ
Tel: 01765 608888

Nearby sights of interest:
Newby Hall; Thorp Perrow Arboretum.

A lead statue of Endymion in front of the Temple of Piety, c1730.

14 *Wallington*

Location: 19km (12 miles) W of Morpeth

Wallington's garden proper lies on the other side of the road from the late 17th-century stone house. Paths lead through woodland which was reputed to have been replanned in the 1760s by "Capability" Brown. It is said that he made the fine lake in the woods and designed the pillared Portico House that overlooks it. After half a mile you come to your goal – the irregular walled former kitchen garden which is now laid out as a pleasure garden. A terraced walk runs down one side with climbing plants and musk roses, and rows of 17th-century Dutch lead figures embellishing the retaining wall. At the end of the walk a conservatory is planted with an exuberant Victorian scheme. The beds below follow no formal pattern but there is clever plant associations everywhere. A National Collection of elders (*Sambucus* spp.) is held here, with over 30 species and cultivars.

開 open: Easter to Oct, daily, 10am–7pm; Nov to Mar, daily, 10am–4pm
open: Easter to end Sep, daily except Tue, 1–5.30pm; Oct, daily except Tue, 1–4.30pm

Further information from:
Cambo, Morpeth, Northumberland
NE61 4AR
Tel: 01670 774283

Nearby sights of interest:
Chesters Fort; Hadrian's Wall; Hexham Abbey.

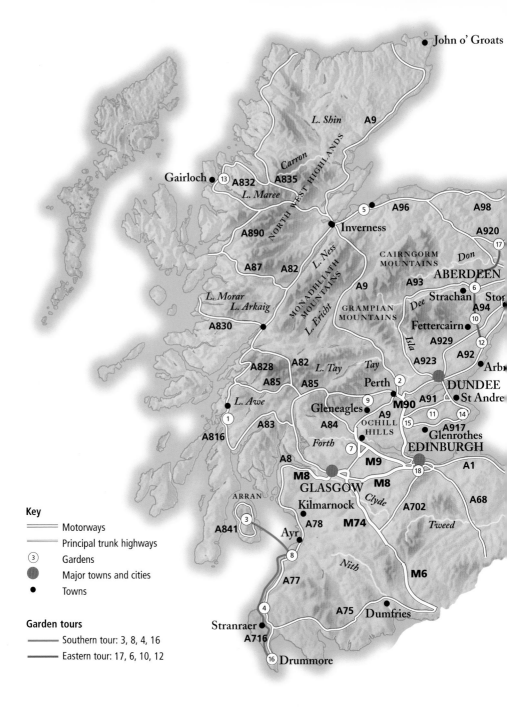

Key

- ═══ Motorways
- ═══ Principal trunk highways
- ③ Gardens
- ● Major towns and cities
- • Towns

Garden tours

- Southern tour: 3, 8, 4, 16
- Eastern tour: 17, 6, 10, 12

Key to gardens

1	Arduaine Gardens	10	Edzell Castle
2	Branklyn Garden	11	Falkland Palace
3	Brodick Castle	12	House of Pitmuies
4	Castle Kennedy Gardens	13	Inverewe
5	Cawdor Castle	14	Kellie Castle
6	Crathes Castle	15	Kinross House
7	Culross Palace	16	Logan Botanic Garden
8	Culzean Castle	17	Pitmedden
9	Drummond Castle	18	Royal Botanic Garden, Edinburgh

Scotland

Until 1603 Scotland was an independent kingdom and
held its own parliament until 1707. Its culture – which
certainly includes gardens – has retained a powerfully
independent character. Historical influences in the
past were more likely to come from France than from
England, especially in the case of gardens. The idea
of aligning the main axis of a garden on some external
feature – a common feature of French gardens – is found
in several 17th-century Scottish gardens. Kinross House
(see p.132) is connected in this way both with the High
Street of the town of Kinross as well as with the ruins of
Loch Leven Castle. Sir William Bruce who designed
both the house and the garden at Kinross House was
among the first foreigners to see the new French gardens
of the 1660s. Pitmedden (see pp.134–137) has much in
common with French garden design of the mid-17th

century – and Bruce was a friend
of its maker. Scotland has always
been receptive to foreign
influence and the crow-stepped
houses of the east coast fishing
villages would scarcely look out
of place on the shores of the
Zuider Zee. There is a lively

The mottled toffee-coloured
bark of an old *Rhododendron
thomsonii* at Inverewe.

spirit of cosmopolitanism in Scottish life, as anyone who has been to the Edinburgh Festival will recognize.

The majority of distinguished Scottish gardens is to be found south of the Caledonian Canal. Historically, the court and the greatest wealth was always in the lowlands and on the east coast. The finest agricultural land – the source of old wealth – is also to be found here. The east coast has much sunshine – East Fife has longer hours of summer sun than anywhere else in Britain. The west coast, where the rainfall may go over 200cm (79in) per annum, strikingly benefits in many places from the balmy effects of the Gulf Stream Drift. Gardens such Arduaine (see p.120), Brodick Castle (see p.122), and Inverewe (see p.130) are thus able to grow remarkable tender rarities, especially plants from the Himalayas.

Scottish gardens show an exceptionally lively use of colour – in tartans and tweeds the Scots show the same subtle but sprightly colour sense as is found in many gardens. Crathes Castle (see p.125), Falkland Palace (see p.128), House of Pitmuies (see p.129), and Pitmedden (see pp.134–7) display a brilliant inventiveness in the deployment of colour. Herbaceous borders here are among the finest in the world, growing with exceptional vigour as a result of the long hours of summer sunshine found so far north.

Scotland is wonderfully rich in plantsman's gardens such as Branklyn (see p.121) near Perth and the west coast gardens like Inverewe. The first director of Kew Gardens, Sir William Hooker, had previously been Professor of Botany at Glasgow University and some of the greatest plant hunters were Scots. The only style of gardening which is scarcely ever found in Scotland is the English-style landscape park. Perhaps with such dramatically beautiful natural scenery such things were thought to be superfluous?

Subtle colour harmonies and the bold shape of a *Prunus lusitanicus* give great character to this border at Crathes Castle.

Arduaine Gardens

Location: 32km (20 miles) S of Oban by A816

open: All year, daily, 9.30am to sunset

Further information from:
Kilmelford, Strathclyde PA34 4XG
Tel: 01852 200366

Nearby sights of interest:
Inveraray Castle; the scenery of the Western Highlands.

Yellow candelabra primulas seem to be quite at home on the banks of a pool.

Arduaine – which is the Gaelic for "green point" – juts out on the southern edge of the opening where Loch Melfort joins the sea. It is a wonderful position, with views over the loch and out towards the Hebridean islands of Shuna and Luing. The climate, with very high rainfall and mild winters, is allied to acid soil to produce the perfect environment for rhododendrons.

The estate was bought in 1898 by James Arthur Campbell, a friend of Osgood Mackenzie, the creator of the gardens at Inverewe (see p.130). Like Mackenzie, it was the position and climate that attracted Campbell for almost nothing grew here and the place is lashed by fierce coastal winds. He chose for his garden a protected hollow at a little distance from the house he built, and planted windbreaks to allow the establishment of the tender plants which would flourish here.

There have been changes of ownership since, and the addition of many new plants. Arduaine now displays superlative trees and shrubs in a setting of unique beauty. It is the tender species rhododendrons that are the most breathtaking sight. Such things as *Rhododendron cinnabarinum* Roylei Group from Sikkim with carmine flowers flecked with purple; the very tender Chinese *R. giganteum* with rich pink flowers and huge leaves; and the white-flowered *R. griffithianum* from the Himalayas. There are also magnificent eucalyptus, griselinias, magnolias, olearias, and much else. All these are grown in naturalistic surroundings, often underplanted with beautiful herbaceous plants – waves of *Narcissus cyclamineus* in spring and, later in the year, unforgettable spreads of intense blue *Meconopsis betonicifolia*.

Arduaine is open all year and in this climate something may burst into flower at any time. Besides, the spectacular evergreen shrubs, some with magnificent leaves like the species rhododendrons, are always thrilling to see.

Branklyn Garden

Location: On the E edge of Perth

open: Mar to Oct, daily, 9.30am to sunset

Further information from:
Dundee Road, Perth, Perthshire
PH2 7BB
Tel: 01738 625535

Nearby sights of interest:
Scone Palace.

This is a most unlikely place to find a garden of consequence, in the genteel suburbs of Perth, up above the busy main road which leads to Dundee. But nothing could be less suburban than this remarkable place and one quickly forgets the roar of traffic. The garden was made by John and Dorothy Renton, who came to live here in 1922. The site is long and slender, gently undulating, with narrow paths running between beds. I call them "beds" but that gives the air of too much contrivance, for they are simply groups of plants. Dorothy Renton's plan from the outset was clear: "There was no preconceived rule of design . . . . It has been evolved gradually and the principle aim has been to give plants the proper conditions – it is primarily a home for plants."

The soil is quite rich and acid, overlaying strata of rock and, unlike the west coast gardens, the rainfall at less than 50cm (20in) per annum is quite modest and the winters can be very harsh. Plants are grouped, following Dorothy Renton's philosophy, in naturalistic combinations. Repeatedly, for example, herbaceous or bulbous plants will find exactly the site in which to thrive in the shade of some shrubs or small trees. This could be something relatively ordinary – a group of pink and cream-yellow azaleas underplanted with blue and white bluebells and Solomon's seal – all flowering at the same time. Other combinations are much more rarefied. A sheet of the exquisite *Fritillaria pallida*, with pink-flushed ivory flowers, surrounded by the gleaming foliage of *Asarum canadense*, spreads out below an old rhododendron. The Japanese maple, *Acer palmatum* 'Rubrum', with thunderously dark foliage, overhangs a little pool about whose banks is a colony of the intense vermilion Turk's cap lily, *Lilium chalcedonicum*. So, although this is primarily a collection of plants, much harmony comes from the juxtaposition of species with similar or complementary needs. Most of the shrubs and trees are of the smaller kinds and with a strong bias for wild species. There are many camellias, euonymus, hebe, pieris, rhododendrons, the smaller willows, and viburnums. Most irresistible of all are the immense riches of smaller herbaceous plants – rare trilliums, Canadian bloodroot, beautiful meconopsis in several different species, many primulas, hellebores, and curious jeffersonias. There are few gardens that display such a wealth of unfamiliar plants in such a small, and beautifully cared for, space.

Species peonies, dazzling blue Himalayan poppies, and rich pink rhododendron.

open: All year, daily, 9.30am to sunset

open: 1–18 Apr, May to Sep, daily, 1–5pm; 19 Apr to 1 May, 2–23 Oct, Mon, Wed and Sat, 1–5pm

Further information from:
Isle of Arran, Strathclyde
KA27 8HY
Tel: 01770 302202

Nearby sights of interest:
The scenery of the Isle of Arran.

Brodick Castle

Location: 3km (2 miles) from Brodick ferry

The Isle of Arran is a beautiful place and Brodick Castle, the ancestral seat of the Dukes of Hamilton, occupies a memorable position high up above Brodick Bay looking across the sea to the Firth of Clyde. Although there was a notable garden here in the early 18th century – the date 1710 is carved in stone above the north door – it is not until the 20th century that the garden became really distinguished. The Duchess of Montrose started to collect rhododendrons just after World War I during an especially brilliant period for plant hunting. Gorge Forrest, Frank Kingdon Ward, Joseph Rock and Reginald Farrer all went on expeditions and made wonderful new discoveries – many of which found their way to Brodick. The very tender Himalayan *Rhododendron maddenii*, with its intensely fragrant white flowers, flourishes here, along with many other species.

The site is an attractively undulating one, well watered, and the picture of vast expanses of Himalayan primulas in late spring, or meconopsis in early summer, spread out before towering old rhododendrons and other distinguished shrubs, is unforgettable. In the middle of the Lower Rhododendron Walk near the shores of Brodick Bay is a delightful Bavarian summerhouse, built to commemorate the marriage of the 10th Duke of Hamilton's son to Princess Marie of Baden. Although there is pretty planting of a more formal character in the walled garden near the castle, it is the naturalistic woodland planting on the slopes between the castle and the sea that provide the distinctive garden experience at Brodick.

In the bog garden red and purple Asiatic primulas flourish alongside the New Zealand flax.

Castle Kennedy Gardens

Location: 8km (5 miles) E of Stranraer by A75

The past is vividly present at Castle Kennedy Gardens. To start with the gardens are disposed in a dramatic landscape that lies between two castles on the estate. To the south are the ruins of the 15th-century Castle Kennedy, ravaged by fire in the early 18th century. At the northern end is the Victorian extravaganza of Lochinch Castle. A distance of 1.5km (1 mile) divides the castles and the garden between is flanked to east and west by the Loch of Inch and Loch Crindl. The most striking historic feature here is the terracing of the ground and the series of radiating walks about a gigantic round pool at the centre. The gardens were laid out by the Earl of Stair in the 1730s. He had been Ambassador to France and, much taken with what he had seen at Versailles, decided to do something on a similarly grand scale. His designer was the architect William Adam who contrived a fascinating mixture of the formal and informal, "Too form'd for Nature – yet too wild for Art" as the poet Samuel Boyse wrote in 1734. This garden was, alas, much altered in a wholescale landscaping which took place between 1799 and 1802, but signs of Adam's garden are still plainly visible. Some restoration of the older garden, using the original plans, was carried out in 1840. The character of the planting today is chiefly of the 19th and 20th centuries. There are imposing groups of rhododendrons and of other ornamental shrubs and conifers. Lively borders light up the old walled garden of the ruined castle. But the distinctive qualities of the gardens here are best understood by taking a long walk in the dramatic landscape that lies between the two lochs and the two castles.

open: Easter to Sep, daily, 10am–5pm

Further information from:
Rephad, Stranraer, Dumfries and Galloway DG9 8BX
Tel: 01776 702024
Fax: 01776 706248

Nearby sights of interest:
The scenery of the Mull of Galloway.

Ebullient mixed borders decorate the walled garden of the ruins of the Medieval castle.

Cawdor Castle

open: May to mid-Oct, daily,
10am–5.30pm
open: As above

Further information from:
Cawdor, Highland IV12 5RD
Tel: 01667 404615
Fax: 01667 404674

Nearby sights of interest:
The Battlefield of Culloden; the
scenery of the Moray Firth.

Location: 17.5km (11 miles) NE of Inverness by A96 and B9090

Macbeth was the most famous Thane of Cawdor but the castle here, although suitably dramatic, was built long after his time. It is a 14th-century fortified tower house, romantic and welcoming rather than forbidding, much added to in the 17th century. It has long been the seat of Campbells, latterly the Earls of Cawdor, and it is this family, right into present times, which has left its mark on the garden.

The old walled garden near the castle has a charming Victorian flavour with grass paths, deep borders in which annuals are intermingled with herbaceous perennials and a rose garden enlivened by the tall shapes of both common, and gold-leaved Irish yew; this part of the garden was laid out by the Lady Cawdor of the day in 1850. Towards the end of the summer the planting in the walled garden assumes astonishing exuberance. In the 19th century many Scottish gardens were planned to be at there most floriferous to delight guests coming for the shooting season. But much of the modern planting here is done with great skill and there are delightful combinations to note and admire: the feathery fronds of a chalk-pink astilbe are interwoven with the trailing stems of soft blue catmint, the curious vivid red mophead flowers of bergamot, *Monarda* 'Cambridge Scarlet', and pale cream *Aconitum* 'Ivorine' rising behind. On one side of the walled garden a gate leads into wonderfully atmospheric woodland. In more recent years entirely new gardens have been added – a paradise garden, a knot garden and a thistle garden. Cawdor is a lively place which manages successfully to preserve the best of its past, and at the same time to give promise for the future.

The walled garden alongside the castle preserves an old-fashioned air immune to whims of fashion.

Crathes Castle

Location: 24km (15 miles) SW of Aberdeen by A93 and 3m E of Banchory

open: All year, daily, 9.30am to sunset
open: Apr to Oct, daily, 11am–6pm

Further information from:
nr Banchory, Grampian AB31 3QJ
Tel: 01330 844525

Nearby sights of interest:
Braemar Castle; salmon fishing and scenery of River Dee.

This is one of Britain's finest gardens, combining ingredients from different periods and weaving them together with great skill. The first known garden design at Crathes survives to this day – one of the oldest extant garden layouts in the country. In the upper garden, immediately south east of the castle, are extraordinary yew hedges and topiary which date back to 1702. The hedges are immensely broad and break out from time to time into giant swirling topiary shapes. They enclose on one side a croquet lawn and on the other the Colour Garden. Four "L"-shaped yew hedges enclose a pool and the surrounding planting is executed in brilliant colours – scarlet nasturtiums, orange-red ligularia, lemon-yellow daylilies, yellow achilleas, and sombre bronze-purple *Berberis thunbergii* f. *atropurpurea*.

The Blue Garden beyond the yew hedge to the east has a Victorian flavour with elaborate geometric bedding schemes of blue annuals and a handsome procession of Portugal laurels (*Prunus lusitanica*) clipped into rounded shapes. South of all this, at a slightly lower level, is the pattern of herbaceous borders which was already established when Gertrude Jekyll visited the garden in 1895: "The brilliancy of colour masses in these Scottish gardens is something remarkable." Modern visitors will be struck in exactly the same way as Miss Jekyll was. This part of the garden is divided into four square areas separated by paths marked at their meeting point by an ancient Portugal laurel with a seat about its trunk. Each section is dominated by a colour scheme – pink and blue, white, yellow and violet, yellow and gold (a trifle bilious, this), and orange and red. The whole area is encircled by mixed borders which are filled with good plants. The Doocot Border, for example, has the Californian evergreen *Umbellularia californica*, the beautiful hydrangea *Hydrangea heteromalla* Bretschneideri Group, a lovely small ash *Fraxinus* x *sieboldiana* and much else that is rare and well chosen.

The 16th-century castle rises high above early 18th-century yew hedges and 20th-century borders.

open: Good Friday to Sep, daily, 11am–5pm
open: As above

Further information from:
Culross, Grampian KY12 8JH
Tel: 01383 880359

Nearby sights of interest;
The town of Culross; Stirling Castle; the Pineapple House (Dunmore).

The recreated 17th-century garden with plants of the period.

7 *Culross Palace*

Location: 22.5km (14 miles) SE of Stirling by A907 and B9037

The first book on Scottish gardening, John Reid's *The Scots Gard'ner*, was not published until 1683, but paintings and surviving evidence on the ground show that Scotland had a thriving tradition of gardening long before that. Culross, an extraordinary enclave of 16th- and 17th-century houses, was established many years before the publication of Reid's book. Culross Palace is scarcely a palace at all – the name arose in a misreading of deeds in the 19th century. It was a prosperous merchant's house, built towards the end of the 16th century for Sir George Bruce.

The land slopes up in terraces behind the house and here a garden of period plants has been laid out. The original garden is most likely to have been a kitchen garden and in its recreation it was decided to restrict plants to what was grown in the 17th

century. The first four beds are of simple turf but roughly cut to give the shaggy appearance of such a thing before the days of mowing machines. Subsequent beds are planted with herbs, fruit and vegetables. Along the side wall is a tunnel arbour with pleached mulberries and grapevines. From the top of the terraced garden the visitor has a most beautiful view of the Firth of Forth seen over the higgledy-piggledy rooftops of the old town.

open: All year, daily, 9.30am to sunset
open: Apr to Oct, daily 10.30am–5.30pm

Further information from:
Maybole, Strathclyde KA19 8LE
Tel: 01655 760274

Nearby sights of interest:
Golf (Turnberry); Glasgow (Burrell Museum, City Museum).

8 *Culzean Castle*

Location: 19km (12 miles) S of Ayr by A719 and 4m SW of Maybole

Culzean Castle is an extraordinary place, a fantasy castellated castle designed by Robert Adam rearing up on the very brim of a plummeting cliff. Created for Sir Thomas Kennedy from 1777 onwards it was, in fact, the remodelling of an earlier house but Adam's work eventually engulfed almost all traces of the past. South of the castle the Fountain Court is a terraced garden with a lily pond and fountain at its centre. The terrace walls give protection to such tender plants as abutilons, myrtles, olearias, the beautiful evergreen winter's bark (*Drimys winteri*), and much else. In the walled former kitchen garden to one side are magnificent deep herbaceous borders, a rose garden and a fine glasshouse.

The woodland is a great feature at Culzean, as it had been in the 19th century. Sir Herbert Maxwell in his book *Scottish Gardens* (1911) describes the purpose of the woodland garden "to devote these glades and glens . . . to hardy exotics set free in a Scottish environment." Distinguished shrubs, especially magnolias and rhododendrons, are underplanted with immense quantities of naturalized bulbs – among them snowdrops, daffodils, and hyacinths. The gardens and park are open every day of the year and in this mild part of Scotland, even in deep winter, something will burst into flower on almost any day of the year.

Drummond Castle

Location: 3km (2 miles) S of Crieff by A822

"The garden at Drummond appears more beautiful than ever . . . . Terrace above terrace with statues and busts of the great men of bygone days placed side by side; flowers of every hue perfuming the air." Thus wrote the artist Jacob Thompson in 1842. Visitors today can see exactly what he saw. Although much of the present appearance of the gardens is 19th century this is misleading, as the underlying layout dates from the early 17th century. The gardens here are, in fact, a remarkable survival of the Scottish Renaissance overlaid with 19th-century planting. In the early 19th century new parterres were made at the foot of the terraces, imposing the pattern of a giant St Andrews cross and adding a profusion of topiary. Clipped *Prunus cerasifera* 'Nigra', junipers, holly, and yew are mixed with fine statues and urns. A central north-south axis unites these elements and the terraces, piercing a gate in the formal garden wall and continuing far into woodland. Queen Victoria came here in 1842 and wrote in her diary: "We walked in the garden which is really very fine, with terraces, like an old French garden."

open: Easter weekend, 2–6pm; May to Oct, daily, 2–6pm

Further information from:
Muthill, nr Crieff, Perthshire
PH7 4HZ
Tel: 01764 681257
Fax: 01764 681550

Nearby sights of interest:
Highland scenery; whisky distilleries.

The Scottish love of exuberant decoration given full rein in the formal garden.

10 *Edzell Castle*

Location: 11km (7 miles) N of Brechin by A90 and B 966

open: Apr to Sep, daily, 9.30am–6pm (Sun, 12 noon to 6pm); Oct to Mar, daily except Fri, 9.30am–4pm (Thu, 9.30am–2pm; Sun, 2–4pm)
open: As above

Further information from:
Brechin, Tayside DD9 7UE
Tel: 01356 648631

Nearby sights of interest:
House of Dun; Fasque.

Renaissance-style formality recreated in the Pleasance.

Edzell was described in the 17th century by the chronicler Ouchterlony of Guinde: "It is ane excellent dwelling, a great house, delicat gardine, with wall sumptuously built of hewen stone." At the beginning of the 17th century the castle was added to by Sir David Lindsay, Lord Edzell, who also created a walled garden, or Pleasance, of great elegance. A pattern of recesses in the red sandstone walls originally contained blue painted boxes of silver-white flowers: the colours of the Lindsay arms. Carved stone panels depicted the planetary deities, the liberal arts, and the essential virtues. There are no longer pots of plants but all these other features survive in a marvellous state of preservation.

The Pleasance was replanted just before World War II as a result of an archaeological exploration of the site. This revealed little, except that there had been an important feature at the centre of the garden. A new garden was laid out which, although quite unhistorical, suits the lively decorativeness of its setting. A yew topiary drum sits on a mound at the centre and a pattern of box-edged beds surrounds it. Here are traced the thistle of Scotland, rose of England and *fleur-de-lys* of France with the Lindsay motto *Dum spiro spero* ("As long as I breathe, I hope").

11 *Falkland Palace*

Location: 17.5km (11 miles) N of Kirkcaldy by A912

open: Good Fri to Oct, Mon to Sat 11am–5.30pm, Sun 1.30–5.30pm
open: As above

Further information from:
Falkland, Fife KY7 7BU
Tel: 01337 857397

Nearby sights of interest:
The town of Falkland, Hill of Tarvit House; St Andrews (golf, cathedral ruins, ancient university).

The MacDuffs lived at Falkland, but its importance chiefly dates from its acquisition in the 14th century by Robert Stewart, the brother of Robert III of Scotland. From the 15th century it was a palace of the Scottish royal family. In the early 16th century King James V married a daughter of François I of France and as a result French masons came to work on the palace. This resulted, in the words of the architectural historian Mark Girouard, in "a display of early Renaissance architecture without parallel in the British Isles."

References to the gardens appear in palace records from time to time but the garden which visitors see today is entirely of the 20th century. After World War II the garden was redesigned and planted by the designer Percy Cane. He took advantage of old stone walls as a background to mixed borders, richly planted with drifts of herbaceous plants. Cane also created free-form island beds, and it was he who had the idea of making a planting of roses symbolizing the heraldic colours of the Stewarts. Since Cane's time additions include a splendid delphinium border.

House of Pitmuies

Location: 11km (7 miles) E of Forfar by A932

open: Easter to Oct, daily, 10am–5pm

Further information from:
Guthrie, by Forfar, Tayside
DD8 2SN
Tel: 01241 828245

Nearby sights of interest:
House of Dun; Glamis Castle.

This is one of the best, and prettiest, private gardens in Scotland. It has a lovely position, much of it enclosed within stone walls, to one side of a beautiful Georgian house. The entrance lies through an old walled kitchen garden in which the decorative and useful are still displayed in the old way. A glasshouse is full of tender plants and the formal *potager* makes a splendid sight. A pattern of raised beds edged in wood contains neat strips of lettuces, carrots, onions and other vegetables and a mulberry, surrounded by ornamental planting, rises in the middle. Decorative planting is intermingled with fruit and vegetables – an apple walk is underplanted with beautiful *Lilium martagon*, both white- and plum-coloured forms, and a rampart of sweet peas rises up among the cabbages.

The kitchen garden goes straight into the flower garden, leading immediately to a long narrow pair of herbaceous borders which form the chief axis. The colour scheme is dominated by white, magenta and pink, with much repetition of plants. The borders are backed by hedges of *Prunus cerasifera* 'Pissardii', cut down each year to encourage rosy-purple new growth. At the far end a gate leads through the wall beyond which is a fine woodland garden on the banks of a stream. To one side a second pair of borders running parallel to the first, is aligned with the drawing room windows and takes its ethereal colour scheme from the decor of the room – soft cream, chalky blue, and white. There are admirable plants everywhere at Pitmuies, used with a lively sense of their decorative potential.

An exciting pattern of colour can be found in this modern plantswoman's garden.

open: mid-Mar to mid-Oct, daily, 9.30am–9pm; mid-Oct to mid-Mar, daily, 9.30am–5pm

Further information from:
Poolewe, Highland IV22 2LQ
Tel: 01445 781200

Nearby sights of interest:
Scenery of the Western Highlands.

Exquisite views of Loch Ewe constantly compete with plants for attention.

Inverewe

Location: 9.5km (6 miles) NE of Gairloch by A832

Inverewe was an extraordinary pioneer among gardens and remains a wonderful place. It was created by Osgood Mackenzie who came here in 1862, finding a beautiful but desolate headland jutting out between the bay of Camas Glas and Loch Ewe. Virtually nothing will grow here without protection from the wind – there was only a solitary willow when Mackenzie arrived. But once there is protection from the wind the very high rainfall and virtually frost-free climate provide an ideal place in which to grow plants. Mackenzie laboured here until he died in 1922 and the great task was continued for a further thirty years by his daughter, Mairi Sawyer. It was taken over by the National Trust for Scotland in 1952.

The garden has the air of a naturalistic jungle, but a jungle found nowhere in nature for it includes plants from all the major plant-growing areas of the southern hemisphere. At the entrance along the drive there are examples of the Tasmanian gum, *Eucalyptus coccifera*, planted by Mackenzie and now over 100 years old. The terrain is attractively undulating but a map is necessary in order not to get lost. There are over 24ha (60 acres) here and the jungle paths resemble each other to a bewildering degree. Here is a huge collection of chiefly species rhododendrons, but there are a few of the better hybrids and cultivars. Australasian plants are well represented – several eucalyptus, but also such things as the Tasmanian tree fern (*Dicksonia antarctica*), myrtles, podocarpus, olearias, and pittosporums. A beautiful collection of magnolias (starting the flowering season in mid-spring with a delicious explosion of *Magnolia campbelli*) includes many of the large-leaved very tender kinds such as the Himalayan *M. globosa*.

In late April or May Inverewe presents its most dazzling display of flowers – greatly enlivened by a cocktail of marvellous scents, not only those of flowers but also the invigorating whiff of eucalyptus foliage. The only gardens that can compare with Inverewe are those of the Cornish coast in south-west England. But Inverewe adds to a very mild climate even greater rainfall than the Cornish gardens, producing plant growth of tropical ebullience.

Kellie Castle

Location: 5km (3 miles) NW of Pittenweem by B9171

open: All year, daily, 9.30am to sunset
open: Apr, Sat and Sun, 2–6pm; May to Sep, daily, 2–6pm

Further information from:
nr Pittenweem, Fife KY10 2RF
Tel: 01333 720271

Nearby sights of interest:
The fishing villages of East Fife (Crail, Anstruther, St Monance, Pittenweem); St Andrews (golf, ruins of cathedral, ancient university).

Kellie Castle has an ancient history – the estate belonged to the Siward family in the 13th century. The present castle was built at various periods from the 14th to the 17th centuries. Starting as a fortified keep as time passed it acquired a more domestic character so that today it presents a positively friendly face. It has a most beautiful position, high up on wooded land which slopes down to the sea of the Firth of Forth.

Its garden history really starts with the castle's acquisition by the Lorimer family in the 19th century. Robert Lorimer was brought up here and from his childhood he took an interest in gardens. As a schoolboy he redesigned the walled garden, strongly influenced by what he took to be the traditional old gardens of Scotland. In a lecture some years later he described the perfect Scottish 17th-century garden: "Great intersecting walks of shaven grass, on either side borders of brightest flowers backed up by low espaliers hanging with shining apples." The walled garden at Kellie still preserves that character. The wall is pierced by a door which opens onto a central walk with an archway covered in 'Dorothy Perkins' roses and a path flanked by herbaceous borders. It is backed by espaliered pears trained on wires. A curvaceous bench, of powerful Arts and Crafts character, forms an eye-catcher at the far end of the garden. There are lawns on either side of the borders and the walls have borders planted with both useful and ornamental plants. It provides a delightful background and above it loom the crow-stepped gables of the castle.

Pale yellow gladioli, roses on an arbour, and an avenue of catmint.

15 *Kinross House*

Location: In the centre of Kinross

open: May to Sep, daily,
10am–7pm

Further information from:
Kinross, Tayside KY13 7ET

Nearby sights of interest:
St Andrews (golf, ruined cathedral,
ancient university); fishing villages
of East Fife.

Box topiary, fine 17th-century
stone walls and a gate of
wrought iron.

Daniel Defoe came to Kinross in 1722 and was greatly impressed with what he saw: ". . . that great architect Sir William Bruce . . . built a noble palace on the banks of this lake [Loch Leven] and adjoining the town of Kinross. This is by much the finest seat I have yet seen in Scotland." House and garden together at Kinross, to this day, present one of the most attractive ensembles in Scotland, with a specifically Scottish character.

Sir William Bruce bought the estate in 1675 and built Kinross House for his own use. From the outset house and garden were conceived together, and when work started in 1679 it was to level the ground for the garden. Bruce's surviving drawings clearly show the essence of the garden layout as it is today. An avenue linked the town of Kinross with the house and this axis continued on the far side of the house, piercing a garden wall on the banks of Loch Leven and "borrowing", as a marvellous eye-catcher, the ruins of Loch Leven castle on an island in the lake. The Bruce family continued at Kinross until the estate passed to the Graham family whose kinsmen, the Montgomerys, live there today. In the late 19th century the house was uninhabited for 80 years until 1902 when Sir Basil Graham-Montgomery restored it, with special attention to the garden. Today, the house is scarcely changed in its essentials from its completion in the 1680s. The central unifying axis is still in place, linking town, house, garden and the castle ruins. The chief ornamental gardens lie between the house and the loch. The ground is terraced with, at the upper level, a rose garden. Steps descend to herbaceous borders and a grass path leads to a wrought-iron gate in the wall through which Loch Leven castle is revealed. The garden is walled and embellished with carved piers and urns. It seems likely that Bruce visited France in the 1660s as the garden is closer to the latest French garden ideas than anything comparable in England of that date. It is a fascinating and enchanting place.

Logan Botanic Garden

Location: 22.5km (14 miles) S of Stranraer by A716

This botanic garden is owned by the Royal Botanic Garden in Edinburgh and may best be thought of as its subtropical outpost. Port Logan lies on a narrow finger of land jutting out into the sea forming the western side of Luce Bay. Warmed by the Gulf Stream Drift, and given humidity by the sea on either side, it is a remarkably privileged site for growing plants. The estate is an ancient one, belonging first to the McDouall family and latterly to the Buchan-Hepburns who started to make a distinguished garden here in the late 19th century. In 1969 the walled garden and some adjacent land was given to the Royal Botanic Garden. The Buchan-Hepburn family remain in the house which is not open to the public.

The garden has two distinct areas – the old walled garden with formal touches and a wilder, woodland garden to one side. The exciting thing in this botanic garden is the excellent collection of tender plants, especially those from the southern hemisphere. Some of these may grow reasonably well in less benign climates but here they may be seen growing in full vigour. New Zealand cabbage palms (*Cordyline australis*), for example, are grown in many other British gardens but here they grow into substantial trees and produce handsome swags of cream flowers with a delicious scent in summer. Many other plants from the southern hemisphere are grown here, including tree ferns (*Dicksonia* species), southern beeches (*Nothofagus*), eucalyptus, and eucryphias. Countless herbaceous plants also provide ornament – Himalayan poppies (*Meconopsis*), several species of diascia, arctotis, sages, the spectacular Chilean *Lobelia tupa*, echiums, and onion scented tulbaghias from South Africa.

The walls support many decorative climbing plants, such as clematis, the sweetly scented trachelospermum, South American mutisia, bomarea, and the Chinese *Cionura erecta*. Although the garden is attractively laid out the chief reason for coming here is to plunge into a world of exotic and rare plants, relishing a climate of subtropical warmth.

open: mid-Mar to Oct, daily, 10am–6pm

Further information from:
Port Logan, Stranraer, Dumfries and Galloway DG9 9ND
Tel: 01776 860231

Nearby sights of interest:
The scenery of the Mull of Galloway.

Clouds of *Erigeron karvinskianus*, intense blue ceanothus, and the bold leaves of tender echiums.

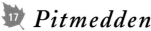

Pitmedden

open: May to Sep, daily,
10am–5.30pm

Further information from:
nr Pitmedden, Ellon,
Aberdeenshire AB4 7PD
Tel: 01651 842352

Nearby sights of interest:
Haddo House; Fyvie Castle;
Leith Hall.

Location: 22.5km (14 miles) N of Aberdeen by A920 and B999

It is very rare that a garden survives after a house is destroyed.
The ancient house at Pitmedden was burnt down in 1818, with
the tragic loss of all its archives, but the garden enclosure, and
enchanting summerhouses and architectural detail – all dating
from the late 17th century – are still there to be seen and
admired. The estate was acquired in 1603 by James Seton whose
family were long distinguished in this part of Scotland. It was his
grandson, Sir Alexander, who made the Great Garden, as it was
called, and his initials together with those of his wife are carved
on the lintel of the entrance to the garden, dated 2nd May 1675.
There are persistent rumours, but no written evidence, that
the garden was designed by the architect and garden designer
Sir William Bruce who was embarking on his new estate at

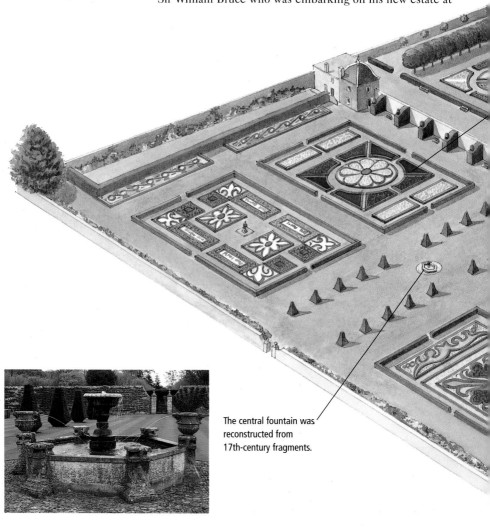

The central fountain was
reconstructed from
17th-century fragments.

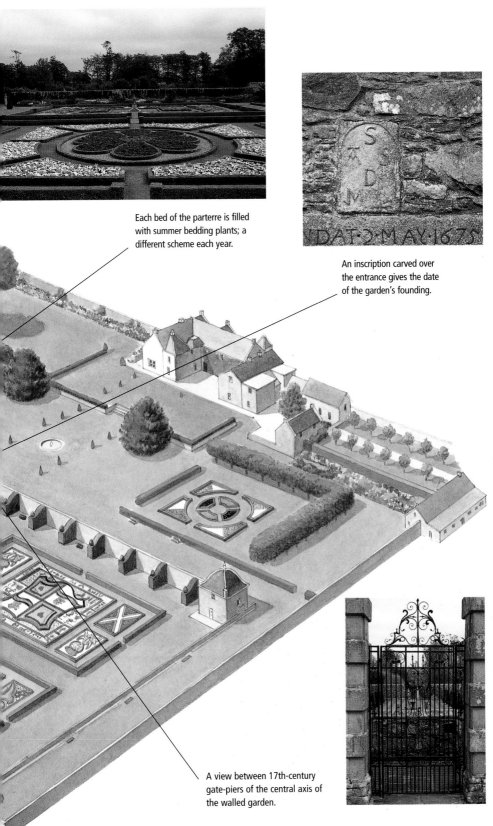

Each bed of the parterre is filled with summer bedding plants; a different scheme each year.

An inscription carved over the entrance gives the date of the garden's founding.

A view between 17th-century gate-piers of the central axis of the walled garden.

Kinross (see p.132) at this time. At all events, this was very much a new-style garden with much in common with the latest French gardens – which Sir William Bruce almost certainly knew.

The Setons retained the Pitmedden estate, building a new house in 1860. The Great Garden was kept up, planted as a large kitchen garden which also contained herbaceous borders. It was a garden much admired by the Arts and Crafts architects of the turn of the century and is included, for example, in H Inigo Triggs's *Formal Gardens in England and Scotland* (1902). It was not until the 1950s, however, when the estate was passed to the National Trust for Scotland that any attempt was made to restore the garden's layout to something appropriate to the splendid formal setting. Dr James Richardson, the architect in charge of the restoration, decided that a symmetrical arrangement would best suit the site. He was inspired by one of the earliest pictures of a Scottish garden: the bird's eye view of the gardens of Holyroodhouse engraved by James Gordon in 1647. He adapted the pattern of formal parterres and designed four giant beds arranged about a central axis with a fountain at its centre. The foundations of this fountain, and some of its stonework, were discovered at the epicentre of the Great Garden. Furthermore, the grand entrance to the garden with its elaborate gate piers and double staircase is in the centre of the wall and aligned with a corresponding gate on the far side of the garden. Indeed, old maps show traces of a continuation of this axis into the woods beyond the garden. This central vista is now emphasized by a broad grass walk with an avenue of yews clipped into obelisks. The beds disposed about it are surrounded by box hedges and each has a different pattern of divisions filled with arabesques or scrolls of clipped box in the tradition of French *parterres de broderie*. The divisions of the parterres are filled with summer bedding plants, of which 60,000 are raised by the garden each year. This is a thoroughly modern style of planting but it has the lively decorative atmosphere that was so characteristic of gardens of the 17th century. Some hedges are clipped to form symbols of words – the words *"Tempus fugit"* surround a beautiful 17th-century multi-facetted sundial and another bed is ornamented with the arms of Seton family together with the Scottish thistle and the St Andrews Cross.

Pale and rich-yellow marigolds, rising exactly to the height of the hedges make a sumptuous scene.

The Great Garden is let into sloping land, with terraces looking down on it on three sides. The view from above of the brilliantly coloured shapes restrained by sombre box hedging is marvellous. The retaining wall on the entrance side of the garden has beautiful 17th-century summerhouses at each end. One of the summerhouses has a curious sundial which tells the time in the afternoon and evening – until 9pm. Scotland has very long summer days and elaborate sundials, covering the whole span of sunlight, and even of moonlight, are a great feature of old Scottish gardens. Dr Richardson had the idea of planting a series of yew buttresses along the wall between the summerhouses. Their tops are clipped into curving shapes, echoing the summerhouses' roofs. The corresponding, west-facing wall, has herbaceous borders which are well done but somehow out of keeping with the sprightly formality of the rest of the garden. Near the entrance to the garden is a tunnel of apples. This is a great fruit-growing part of Scotland and some of the varieties grown are those known from the 17th century such as 'Calville Rouge d'Hiver', 'Golden Reinette', and 'Catshead'.

Some garden historians have criticized Pitmedden for its mixture of garden styles, but we do not know exactly what any 17th-century Scottish garden looked like. Here the architectural setting has been brilliantly used as the background to a layout which successfully honours the decorative spirit of the past.

Shaped buttresses of yew are capped with clipped pinecones.

A view across the pattern of parterres showing the central avenue of yew pyramids.

137

open: Nov to Feb, daily,
10am–4pm (closes 25 Dec and
1 Jan); Mar to Apr, daily,
10am–6pm; May to Aug, daily,
10am–8pm; Sep to Oct, daily,
10am–6pm

Further information from:
Inverleith Row, Edinburgh EH3 5LR
Tel: 0131 5527171
Fax: 0131 5520382

Nearby sights of interest:
Edinburgh (National Gallery,
Museum of Modern Art, Royal
Scottish Museum, Scottish
National Portrait Gallery, New
Town, Royal Mile, Palace of
Holyroodhouse).

**The rock garden displays
an astonishing range of
alpine plants.**

18 *Royal Botanic Garden, Edinburgh*

Location: 1.5km (1 mile) N of the centre of Edinburgh

Like other botanic gardens Edinburgh is primarily a botanical research institution but its garden is of quite special interest to gardeners. Its immense and beautiful collection is rich in ornamental plants, it is exceptionally attractively laid out and, in addition, it has displays of a specifically horticultural kind. The garden was founded in 1670, second in Britain only to Oxford Botanic Garden (see p.86). It was started by the university department of medicine to grow medicinal plants. The collection was moved to its present site in 1820 since when it has expanded enormously. It has a hilly position, high and airy with magnificent views – to the skyline of Edinburgh to the south and to the Firth of Forth and the hills of Fife to the north. Paths wind about the hill with marvellous specimen trees disposed on lawns.

Several collections are devoted to specific environments, for example a peat garden, woodland garden, heath and rock garden. This last is one of the finest examples in the country with narrow paths and precipitous steps leading between rocky outcrops. It

contains a collection of beautifully grown plants including many rarities, such as species of fritillaries and trilliums, which flourish particularly well in this climate. The arboretum forms a great crescent about the south-facing contours of the hill and is especially rich in shrubs and trees from China. On the northern side of the hills are many rhododendrons and azaleas. All this covers a large area – well over 24ha (60 acres) – in which no gardener, however expert could fail to find things of beauty and interest.

The purely horticultural aspect of the garden is shown in the demonstration garden which displays, for example, a splendid range of impeccable hedges each made of a different plant, and between each a border showing the use of a particular group of plants. Lastly, beautiful glasshouses contain non-hardy plants, among them succulents, aquatic plants from warm temperate climates, temperate plants, ferns, and orchids. The garden is well kept and immensely popular with Edinburgh inhabitants.

Glossary

Arcadia (Greek) An idealized rural scene of simple pleasure and peace. Originally a pastoral region of Ancient Greece.

Arts and Crafts A group of artists and craftsmen – including John Ruskin and William Morris – who influenced English garden designers such as Gertrude Jekyll whose gardens are characterized by the use of local building materials and traditional plants and the rejection of the regimented artificiality of much Victorian planting.

bosquet (French) A formal grove, often with a decorative glade in which statues or other ornaments may be placed.

beau idéal (French) The perfect model or type. Literally "beautiful ideal".

Bloomsbury Group A group of English artists and writers active in Bloomsbury, London, including Virginia Woolf, Clive and Vanessa Bell, and Lytton Strachey.

Chinoiserie (French) A Chinese fashion in the decorative arts, especially popular in England and Germany in the 18th century, fostered by trading contacts with the Far East.

claire-voyée (French) An opening in a hedge or wall allowing a view of what lies beyond. Often framed with ornamental supports or light railings.

Doric (Greek) The oldest and simplest of the three Ancient Greek orders of architecture dating back to the 7th century BC.

exedra (Greek) An ornamental, open garden building which is often curved with a bench inside.

ferme ornée (French) Literally, "ornamental farm". A small rustic building, often thatched, which is used as a picturesque feature in a landscape garden.

fleur-de-lys (French) A conventionalized iris flower with three petals, often an emblem in art and heraldry, which is particularly associated with the royal house of France.

International Modern Functional design using modern materials and avoiding traditional elements.

Palladian A style of architecture, popular in Britain in the 18th century which was based on Greek and Roman principles, as reinterpreted by Andrea Palladio, a 16th-century Italian architect.

parterre (French) A formal bedding with low hedges, often of box, disposed in a regular way and often incorporating topiary, urns, or other decorative devices.

parterre de broderie (French) A particular form of parterre in which the shapes of the box hedges are arranged in long flowing patterns which imitate embroidery patterns.

potager (French) Kitchen garden, usually formal or decorative.

putti (Italian) Ornamental cherubs, especially associated with Baroque architecture, painting, and gardens.

Rococo (Italian) Style of architecture made distinct by curved forms and elaborate decoration.

Biographies

Bridgeman, Charles (d1738) Pioneer English landcape designer who was responsible for Blenheim, Rousham, and Wimpole Hall.

Brown, "Capability" Lancelot (1716–83) Landscape gardener and architect who designed the grounds at Kew and Blenheim. He collaborated with William Kent and Henry Holland.

Cane, Percy (1881–1976) Garden designer who often laid out informal beds in formal settings. He was responsible for the new borders at Falkland Palace.

Evelyn, John (1620–1706) English diarist who settled at Sayes Court, Deptford in 1620. He wrote a famous work on sylviculture, *Sylva, or a Discourse of Forest-Trees*, in 1664 and did a great deal to improve horticulture and introduce exotic species to England.

Jekyll, Gertrude (1843–1932) Artist, writer, and garden designer who worked in collaboration with Edwin Lutyens. She designed Hestercombe and many other gardens and wrote several celebrated books, including *Wood and Garden* in 1899.

Jellicoe, Sir Geoffery (1900–) Landscape architect and designer who worked at Pusey House and Ditchley Park amongst others.

Jones, Inigo (1573–1652) Architect and painter who was the first to introduce pure Renaissance architecture from Italian ideas, especially those of Palladio. He laid out gardens at Lincoln's Inn and Wilton House, in collaboration with Isaac de Caus.

Kent, William (1658–1748) Architect, decorator, and celebrated landscape gardener who worked at Rousham, Stowe, and Claremont.

Le Nôtre, André (1613–1700) French landscape architect, often considered to be the most important designer of the Baroque period. He laid out gardens at Vaux-le-Vicomte for Nicolas Fouquet, and at Versailles for Louis XIV.

Lloyd, Christopher (1921–) Gardener, writer of several influential books, and custodian of Great Dixter.

London, George (d1714) Garden designer and nurseryman who worked closely with Henry Wise. He designed parts of the gardens at Blenheim, Chatsworth, Castle Howard, and Longleat. His entire garden layout still survives at Melbourne Hall.

Lutyens, Sir Edwin (1869–1944) Architect and garden designer who worked with Gertrude Jekyll. He laid out gardens at Hestercombe, Folly Farm, and New Delhi amongst others.

Nash, John (1752–1835) Architect who designed many buildings and towns in a range of different styles, including Regent Street, Regent's Park, Clarence House, and Carlton House Terrace.

Paxton, Sir Joseph (1803–65) Architect and garden designer who was responsible for areas of Tatton Park, Chatsworth, Lismore in Ireland, and Château de Ferrières in France.

Peto, Harold (1854–1933) Architect and designer who was influenced by the Italian formal garden.

Repton, Humphry (1752–1818) Landscape designer responsible for Sheffield Park, Sheringham, Tatton, Woburn Abbey, and many others.

Robinson, William (1838–1935) Irish gardener and writer of the influential *The English Flower Garden* (1883). He was a supporter of "wild" gardening and has had an influence on woodland and natural garden styles.

Roper, Lanning (1912–83) American landscape designer who worked extensively in Britain and Ireland.

Index

Acknowledgements

I received much help from garden owners all over Britain – I am most grateful to them all. Many kind friends made suggestions of places to visit which were immensely helpful. At my publisher I have very much appreciated the advice, help and friendliness of Jane Aspden, Guy Croton, Michèle Byam, Selina Mumford, and Anna Nicholas. My wife, Caroline, has been a marvellous help in every way, as always.

Patrick Taylor, *September 1997*

Photographic acknowledgments

Front jacket: Garden Matters.
Back jacket: Robert Harding Picture Library c. Jerry Harpur
b National Trust Photographic Library/Ian Shaw t
Inside back flap: Caroline Taylor

t=top; b=bottom; c=centre

The Edinburgh Photographic Library /Davenport 235 tl. EXPLORER /Nicholson/R. Harding 36 t. Garden Matters /Ken Gibson 66, 107. John Glover 67. Robert Harding Picture Library /John Miller 36 b, /Nigel Temple 84. Dennis Hardley 1, 120. Jerry Harpur 9 t, 27, 52 b, 53 t, 54 b, 59 bl, 59 br, 61 b, 62. John Heseltine 34. Andrew Lawson Photography 2, 3, 14, 15, 17, 20, 21, 29, 33, 60, 95, 104, 105, 129, /Christopher Lloyd 54 t. S & O Mathews 101. National Trust Photographic Library /Andrew Lawson 5, /Nick Meers 37 t, 38, /Stephen Robson 9 b, 25, 46, 87, /Ian Shaw 69, 79, /Rupert Truman 95, 97 t. National Trust for Scotland Photo Library 121. Clive Nichols Photography 39, 73, 90, 92. Hugh Palmer 8, 10 11, 28, 51, 53 b, 61 t, 81, 85, 96, 100, 106, 114, 128. Reed Consumer Books Limited. /Stephen Robson 26, 44, 45. Still Moving Picture Company 124, /Glyn Satterley 136. Patrick Taylor 13, 18, 19, 22, 23, 30, 31, 32, 35, 37 b, 40, 41, 43, 47, 49, 50, 52 t, 55 b, 56, 57, 58, 59 t, 63, 64, 70, 71, 77, 78, 80, 82, 83, 86, 88, 91, 93, 94, 95, 97 b, 98, 99, 103, 108, 109, 110, 111, 112, 113, 115,, 117, 118 119, 122, 123, 125, 126, 130, 131, 132, 133, 134, 135 tr, 135 b, 137 t, 137 b, 138. Travel Ink /Ian Booth 7, /David Toase 89. Steve Wooster 24, 48, 55 t, 65, 68, 74 75, 127.